SELECTIONS
FROM THE WRITINGS
OF THE BÁB

Selections from the
Writings of

THE BÁB

*Compiled by the Research Department of
the Universal House of Justice
and translated by*

HABIB TAHERZADEH

*with the assistance of a Committee
at the Bahá'í World Centre*

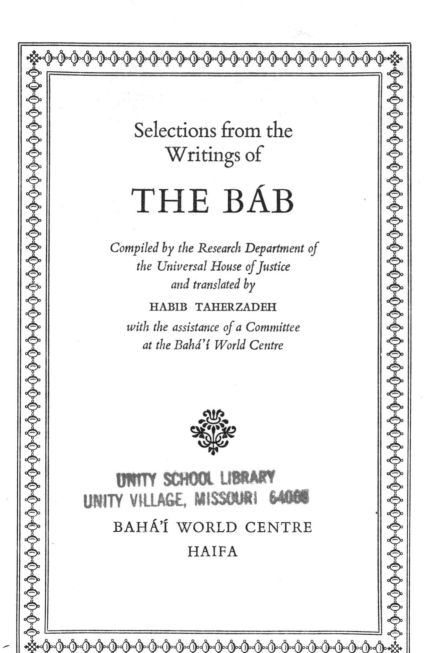

BAHÁ'Í WORLD CENTRE

HAIFA

ISBN 0 85398 066 7

12/97

SET IN 13 ON 14 PT 'MONOTYPE' BEMBO AND
PRINTED IN GREAT BRITAIN
BY W & J MACKAY LIMITED, CHATHAM

PREFACE

The Bahá'í Community has long awaited the day when a comprehensive selection from the writings of the Báb would be made available to it. Ever since Shoghi Effendi translated and published Nabíl's Narrative, and set forth in his monumental works the exalted station of the Báb, the Bahá'ís the world over, and particularly those in the West, have, in their longing to draw nearer to the glorious spirit of Him Who was not only the Herald of their Faith but the Bearer of an independent Revelation, eagerly anticipated an authentic compilation of His revealed utterances and writings. This volume, it is hoped, will be an initial and effective step in that direction.

In view of the vastness of the writings of the Báb, a thorough review of His several works was required. The Universal House of Justice entrusted this task to its Research Department. The actual translation was made by Mr. Habib Taherzadeh, who for several years himself served in that Department. With the assistance of a committee which worked with him, this work is now completed, and it is being made available to Bahá'ís and the general public as a precious addition to the volume of Bahá'í literature in the English language.

References to the Qur'án

In footnotes referring to the Qur'án the súrihs have been numbered according to the original, whereas the verse numbers are those in Rodwell's translation which differ sometimes from those of the Arabic.

CONTENTS

vii

1

TABLETS AND ADDRESSES

A TABLET ADDRESSED TO
'HIM WHO WILL BE MADE MANIFEST'

This is an epistle from this lowly servant to the All-Glorious Lord—He Who hath been aforetime and will be hereafter made manifest. Verily He is the Most Manifest, the Almighty.

IN the name of the Sovereign Lord, the Lord of Power.

Glorified is He before Whom all the dwellers of earth and heaven bow down in adoration and unto Whom all men turn in supplication. He is the One Who holdeth in His grasp the mighty kingdom of all created things and unto Him shall all return. He is the One Who revealeth whatsoever He willeth and by His injunction 'Be Thou' all things have come into being.

This is an epistle from the letter 'Thá'[1] unto Him Who will be made manifest through the power of Truth—He Who is the All-Glorious, the Best Beloved—to affirm that all created things as well as myself bear witness for all time that there is none other God but Thee, the Omnipotent, the Self-Subsisting; that Thou art God, there is no God besides Thee and that all men shall be raised up to life through Thee.

Lauded and glorified be Thy name, O Lord, my God!

[1] This is the first letter of 'Thamarih' which means 'fruit'. Shoghi Effendi, in his writings, refers to the Báb as the 'Thamarih' (fruit) of the Tree of God's successive Revelations. (See Shoghi Effendi's letter to the Bahá'ís of the East dated Naw-Rúz 110, page 5.)

From all eternity I have indeed recognized Thee and unto all eternity will ever do so through Thine Own Self and not through any one else besides Thee. Verily Thou art the Source of all knowledge, the Omniscient. From everlasting I have besought and unto everlasting will beseech forgiveness for my limited understanding of Thee, aware as I am that there is no God but Thee, the All-Glorious, the Almighty.

I beg of Thee, O my Best Beloved, to pardon me and those who earnestly seek to promote Thy Cause; Thou art indeed the One Who forgiveth the sins of all mankind. And in this second year of my Revelation—a Revelation which took place at Thy behest—I bear witness that Thou art the Most Manifest, the Omnipotent, the Ever-Abiding; that of all things that exist on earth and in the heavens nothing whatsoever can frustrate Thy purpose and that Thou art the Knower of all things and the Lord of might and majesty.

Verily, we have believed in Thee and in Thy signs ere the dawn of Thy Manifestation, and in Thee are we all well-assured. Verily, we have believed in Thee and in Thy signs after the fulfilment of Thy Manifestation, and in Thee do we all believe. Verily, we have believed in Thee and in Thy signs at the hour of Thy Manifestation and bear witness that through Thine injunction 'Be Thou' all things have been created.

Every Manifestation is but a revelation of Thine Own Self, with each of Whom we have truly appeared and we bow down in adoration before Thee. Thou hast been, O my Best Beloved, and shalt ever be my witness throughout bygone times and in the days to come. Verily, Thou art the All-Powerful, the Ever-Faithful, the Omnipotent.

I have testified to Thy oneness through Thine Own Self

before the dwellers of the heavens and the earth, bearing witness that, verily, Thou art the All-Glorious, the Best Beloved. I have attained the recognition of Thee through Thine Own Self before the dwellers of the heavens and the earth, bearing witness that Thou art in truth the Almighty, the All-Praised. I have glorified Thy Name through Thine Own Self before the dwellers of the heavens and the earth, bearing witness that Thou art indeed the Lord of power, He Who is the Most Manifest. I have exalted Thy holiness through Thine Own Self before the dwellers of the heavens and the earth, bearing witness that in truth Thou art the Most Sanctified, the Most Holy. I have praised Thy sanctity through Thine Own Self before the dwellers of the heavens and the earth, bearing witness that Thou art indeed the Indescribable, the Inaccessible, the Immeasurably Glorified. I have extolled Thine overpowering majesty through Thine Own Self before the dwellers of the heavens and the earth, bearing witness that, verily, Thou and Thou alone art the Lord of might, the Eternal One, the Ancient of Days.

Hallowed and glorified art Thou; there is none other God but Thee and in truth unto Thee do we all return.

As to those who have put the kindred of 'Alí to death, ere long they shall realize to what depths of perdition they have descended.

*May the glances of Him Whom God shall make manifest
illumine this letter at the primary school.*[1]

He is the Most Glorious.

H E is God, no God is there but Him, the Almighty, the
Best Beloved. All that are in the heavens and on the earth
and whatever lieth between them are His. Verily He is the
Help in Peril, the Self-Subsisting.

This is a letter from God, the Help in Peril, the Self-
Subsisting, unto God, the Almighty, the Best Beloved, to

[1] In one of His Tablets 'Abdu'l-Bahá explains that some were mis-
led by this statement and thought that the school referred to was
a physical school for the training of unlettered children, whereas
it referred to a spiritual school sanctified from the limits of the
contingent world. Bahá'u'lláh in the *Kitáb-i-Aqdas* also refers to
this Epistle of the Báb in the following words:

*O Thou Supreme Pen! Move over the Tablet by the leave of Thy
Lord, the Creator of the heavens. Call Thou then to mind the day when
the Fountainhead of divine unity sought to attend the school which is
sanctified of all save God, that perchance the righteous might become
acquainted, to the extent of a needle's eye, with that which is concealed
behind the veil of the inner mysteries of Thy Lord, the Almighty, the
All-Knowing.*

*Say, We, in truth, entered the school of inner meaning and exposi-
tion at a time when the minds of all that dwell on earth were wrapt in
heedlessness. We beheld what the Merciful Lord had revealed, accepted
the gift He [the Báb] had offered Me of the verses of God, the Help in
Peril, the Self-Subsisting, and hearkened to that to which He had*

affirm that the Bayán and such as bear allegiance to it are but a present from me unto Thee and to express my undoubting faith that there is no God but Thee, that the kingdoms of Creation and Revelation are Thine, that no one can attain anything save by Thy power and that He Whom Thou hast raised up is but Thy servant and Thy Testimony, begging to address Thee by Thy leave in these words: 'Shouldst Thou dismiss the entire company of the followers of the Bayán in the Day of the Latter Resurrection by a mere sign of Thy finger even while still a suckling babe, Thou wouldst indeed be praised in Thy indication. And though no doubt is there about it, do Thou grant a respite of nineteen years as a token of Thy favour so that those who have embraced this Cause may be graciously rewarded by Thee. Thou art verily the Lord of grace abounding. Thou dost indeed suffice every created thing and causest it to be independent of all things, while nothing in the heavens or

---

attested in the Tablet. We, verily, are the Witness. We responded to His call at Our Own behest, and We are, in truth, the Ordainer.

O people of the Bayán! We entered the School of God when ye were slumbering on your couches, and perused the Tablet when ye were fast asleep. By the righteousness of God, the True One, We had read it before it was revealed, and ye were utterly unaware. Indeed Our knowledge had encompassed the Book when ye were yet unborn.

These utterances are revealed according to your measure, not to God's, and unto this beareth witness that which is enshrined in the knowledge of God, did ye but know. Unto this testifieth He Who is the Mouthpiece of God, could ye but understand. By the righteousness of God! Were We to lift the veil ye would swoon away. Take heed lest ye dispute with Him and His Cause. He hath indeed appeared in such wise as to encompass all things, whether of the past or of the future. Were We to speak forth at this time in the language of the dwellers of the Kingdom, We would say that God raised up this School ere the earth and the heavens were brought into being, and We entered it before the letters 'B' and 'E' were joined and knit together.

on the earth or that which lieth between them can ever suffice Thee.'

Verily Thou art the Self-Sufficient, the All-Knowing; Thou art indeed potent over all things.

This is that which We have revealed for the First Believer in Him Whom God shall make manifest, that it may serve as an admonition from Our presence unto all mankind.

In the Name of the Almighty, the Best Beloved.

LAUDED and glorified is He Who is the sovereign Lord of the kingdoms of heaven and earth and whatever is between them. Say, verily unto Him shall all return, and He is the One Who guideth at His Own behest whomsoever He pleaseth. Say, all men beseech His blessings and He is supreme over all created things. He is indeed the All-Glorious, the Mighty, the Well-Beloved.

This is an epistle from the letter 'Thá' unto him who is the First Believer. Bear thou witness that verily He is I, Myself, the Sovereign, the Omnipotent. He is the One Who ordaineth life and death and unto Him shall all return. Indeed there is none other God but Him and all men bow down in adoration before Him. Verily Thy Lord, God, shall presently recompense every one as He ordaineth, even swifter than uttering the words 'Be thou, and it is'.

God hath in truth testified in His Book and so also have testified the company of His angels, His Messengers and those endued with divine knowledge, that thou hast believed in God and in His signs and that everyone is guided aright by virtue of thy guidance. This is indeed a boundless grace which God, the Ever-Living, the Self-Subsisting, hath graciously conferred upon thee aforetime and will confer hereafter. And since thou didst believe in God before the creation, He hath in truth, at His own behest, raised thee up in every Revelation. There is no God but Him, the Sovereign Protector, the All-Glorious.

It behooveth you to proclaim the Cause of God unto all created things as a token of grace from His presence; no God is there but Him, the Most Generous, the All-Compelling.

Say: All matters must be referred to the Book of God; I am indeed the First to believe in God and in His signs; I am the One Who divulgeth and proclaimeth the Truth and I have been invested with every excellent title of God, the Mighty, the Incomparable. Verily I have attained the Day of the First Manifestation and by the bidding of the Lord and as a token of His grace, I shall attain the Day of the Latter Manifestation. There is no God but Him and at the appointed hour everyone shall bow down unto Him in adoration.

I render thanks and yield praise unto God for having been chosen by Him as the Exponent of His Cause in by-gone days and in the days to come; there is none other God save Him, the Glorified, the All-Praised, the Ever-Abiding. Whatever is in the heavens and on the earth is His and through Him are we guided aright.

O people of the Bayán! Those who embrace the Truth must turn unto Me, as ordained in the Book and divine guidance will be vouchsafed to whosoever attaineth My presence.

EXTRACTS FROM AN EPISTLE TO
MUḤAMMAD SHÁH

THE substance wherewith God hath created Me is not the clay out of which others have been formed. He hath conferred upon Me that which the worldly-wise can never comprehend, nor the faithful discover . . . I am one of the sustaining pillars of the Primal Word of God. Whosoever hath recognized Me, hath known all that is true and right, and hath attained all that is good and seemly; and whosoever hath failed to recognize Me, hath turned away from all that is true and right and hath succumbed to everything evil and unseemly.

I swear by the righteousness of Thy Lord, the Lord of all created things, the Lord of all the worlds! Were a man to rear in this world as many edifices as possible and worship God through every virtuous deed which God's knowledge embraceth, and attain the presence of the Lord, and were he, even to a measure less than that which is accountable before God, to bear in his heart a trace of malice towards Me, all his deeds would be reduced to naught and he would be deprived of the glances of God's favour, become the object of His wrath and assuredly perish. For God hath ordained that all the good things which lie in the treasury of His knowledge shall be attained through obedience unto Me, and every fire recorded in His Book, through disobedience unto Me. Methinks in this day and from this station I behold all those who cherish My love and follow My behest abiding within the mansions of Paradise, and the entire company of Mine adversaries consigned to the lowest depths of hell-fire.

By My life! But for the obligation to acknowledge the Cause of Him Who is the Testimony of God . . . I would not have announced this unto thee . . . All the keys of heaven God hath chosen to place on My right hand, and all the keys of hell on My left . . .

I am the Primal Point from which have been generated all created things. I am the Countenance of God Whose splendour can never be obscured, the Light of God Whose radiance can never fade. Whoso recognizeth Me, assurance and all good are in store for him, and whoso faileth to recognize Me, infernal fire and all evil await him . . .

I swear by God, the Peerless, the Incomparable, the True One: for no other reason hath He—the supreme Testimony of God—invested Me with clear signs and tokens than that all men may be enabled to submit to His Cause.

By the righteousness of Him Who is the Absolute Truth, were the veil to be lifted, thou wouldst witness on this earthly plane all men sorely afflicted with the fire of the wrath of God, a fire fiercer and greater than the fire of hell, with the exception of those who have sought shelter beneath the shade of the tree of My love. For they in very truth are the blissful . . .

God beareth Me witness, I was not a man of learning, for I was trained as a merchant. In the year sixty[1] God graciously infused my soul with the conclusive evidences and weighty knowledge which characterize Him Who is the Testimony of God—may peace be upon Him—until finally in that year I proclaimed God's hidden Cause and unveiled its well-guarded Pillar, in such wise that no one could refute it. 'That he who should perish might perish

[1] 1260 A.H. (1844 A.D.)

with a clear proof before him and he who should live might live by clear proof.'[1]

In that same year [year 60] I despatched a messenger and a book unto thee, that thou mightest act towards the Cause of Him Who is the Testimony of God as befitteth the station of thy sovereignty. But inasmuch as dark, dreadful and dire calamity had been irrevocably ordained by the Will of God, the book was not submitted to thy presence, through the intervention of such as regard themselves the well-wishers of the government. Up to the present, when nearly four years have passed, they have not duly presented it to Your Majesty. However, now that the fateful hour is drawing nigh, and because it is a matter of faith, not a worldly concern, therefore I have given thee a glimpse of what hath transpired.

I swear by God! Shouldst thou know the things which in the space of these four years have befallen Me at the hands of thy people and thine army, thou wouldst hold thy breath from fear of God, unless thou wouldst rise to obey the Cause of Him Who is the Testimony of God and make amends for thy shortcomings and failure.

While I was in Shíráz the indignities which befell Me at the hands of its wicked and depraved Governor waxed so grievous that if thou wert acquainted with but a tithe thereof, thou wouldst deal him retributive justice. For as a result of his unmitigated oppression, thy royal court hath become, until the Day of Resurrection, the object of the wrath of God. Moreover, his indulgence in alcohol had grown so excessive that he was never sober enough to make a sound judgement. Therefore, disquieted, I was obliged to set out from Shíráz with the aim of attaining the enlightened and exalted court of Your Majesty. The

[1] Qur'án 8:44

Mu'tamidu'd-Dawlih then became aware of the truth of the Cause and manifested exemplary servitude and devotion to His chosen ones. When some of the ignorant people in his city arose to stir up sedition, he defended the divine Truth by affording Me protection for a while in the privacy of the Governor's residence. At length, having attained the good-pleasure of God, he repaired to his habitation in the all-highest Paradise. May God reward him graciously . . .

Following his ascension to the eternal Kingdom, the vicious Gurgín, resorting to all manner of treachery, false oaths and coercion, sent Me away from Iṣfáhán with an escort of five guards on a journey which lasted seven days, without providing the barest necessities for My travel (Alas! Alas! for the things which have touched Me!), until eventually Your Majesty's order came, instructing Me to proceed to Mákú . . .

I swear by the Most Great Lord! Wert thou to be told in what place I dwell, the first person to have mercy on Me would be thyself. In the heart of a mountain is a fortress [Mákú] . . . the inmates of which are confined to two guards and four dogs. Picture, then, My plight . . . I swear by the truth of God! Were he who hath been willing to treat Me in such a manner to know Who it is Whom he hath so treated, he, verily, would never in his life be happy. Nay—I, verily, acquaint thee with the truth of the matter—it is as if he hath imprisoned all the Prophets, and all the men of truth and all the chosen ones . . .

When this decree was made known unto Me, I wrote to him who administereth the affairs of the kingdom, saying: 'Put Me to death, I adjure thee by God, and send My head wherever thou pleasest. For surely an innocent person such as I, cannot reconcile himself to being consigned to a place reserved for criminals and let his life continue.' My plea remained unanswered. Evidently His Excellency the Ḥájí, is not fully aware of the truth of our Cause. It would be far more heinous a deed to sadden the hearts of the faithful, whether men or women, than to lay waste the sacred House of God.

Verily, the One True God beareth Me witness that in this Day I am the true mystic Fane of God, and the Essence of all good. He who doeth good unto Me, it is as if he doeth good unto God, His angels and the entire company of His loved ones. He who doeth evil unto Me, it is as if he doeth evil unto God and His chosen ones. Nay, too exalted is the station of God and of His loved ones for any person's good or evil deed to reach their holy threshold. Whatever reacheth Me is ordained to reach Me; and that which hath come unto Me, to him who giveth will it revert. By the One in Whose hand is My soul, he hath cast no one but himself into prison. For assuredly whatsoever God hath decreed for Me shall come to pass and naught else save that which God hath ordained for us shall ever touch us. Woe betide him from whose hands floweth evil, and blessed the man from whose hands floweth good. Unto no one do I take My plaint save to God; for He is the best of judges. Every state of adversity or bliss is from Him alone, and He is the All-Powerful, the Almighty.

In brief, I hold within My grasp whatsoever any man might wish of the good of this world and of the next. Were I to remove the veil, all would recognize Me as their Best Beloved, and no one would deny Me. Let not this assertion astound Your Majesty; inasmuch as a true believer in the unity of God who keepeth his eyes directed towards Him alone, will regard aught else but Him as utter nothingness. I swear by God! I seek no earthly goods from thee, be it as much as a mustard seed. Indeed, to possess anything of this world or of the next would, in My estimation, be tantamount to open blasphemy. For it ill beseemeth the believer in the unity of God to turn his gaze to aught else, much less to hold it in his possession. I know of a certainty that since I have God, the Ever-Living, the Adored One, I am the possessor of all things, visible and invisible . . .

In this mountain I have remained alone, and have come to such a pass that none of those gone before Me have suffered what I have suffered, nor any transgressor endured what I have endured! I render praise unto God and yet again praise Him. I find Myself free from sorrow, inasmuch as I abide within the good-pleasure of My Lord and Master. Methinks I am in the all-highest Paradise, rejoicing at My communion with God, the Most Great. Verily this is a bounty which God hath conferred upon Me; and He is the Lord of unbounded blessings.

I swear by the truth of God! Wert thou to know that which I know, thou wouldst forgo the sovereignty of this world and of the next, that thou mightest attain My good-pleasure, through thine obedience unto the True One . . . Wert thou to refuse, the Lord of the world would raise up one who would exalt His Cause, and the Command of God would, verily, be carried into effect.

Through the grace of God nothing can frustrate My purpose, and I am fully conscious of that which God hath bestowed upon Me as a token of His favour. If it were My will, I would disclose to Your Majesty all things; but I have not done this, nor will I do it, that the Truth may be distinguished from aught else beside it, and this prophecy uttered by the Imám Báqir—may peace rest upon Him —be fully realized: 'What must needs befall us in Ádhirbáyján is inevitable and without parallel. When this happeneth, rest ye in your homes and remain patient as we have remained patient. As soon as the Mover moveth make ye haste to attain unto Him, even though ye have to crawl over the snow.'

I implore pardon of God for Myself and for all things related to Me and affirm, 'Praise be to God, the Lord of all the worlds'.

GLORY be unto Him Who knoweth all that is in the heavens and in the earth. Verily there is no God but Him, the sovereign Ruler, the Almighty, the Great.

He is the One Who on the Day of Severing shall pass judgement through the power of Truth; indeed no God is there besides Him, the Peerless, the All-Compelling, the Exalted. He is the One Who holdeth within His grasp the kingdom of all created things; there is none other God but Him, the Single, the Incomparable, the Ever-Abiding, the Inaccessible, the Most Great.

At this moment I testify unto God, even as He testified unto Himself before the creation of all things: Verily there is no God save Him, the All-Glorious, the All-Wise. And I bear witness unto whatsoever He hath fashioned or will fashion, even as He Himself, in the majesty of His glory, hath borne witness: No God is there but Him, the Peerless, the Self-Subsisting, the Most Wondrous.

In God, Who is the Lord of all created things, have I placed My whole trust. There is no God but Him, the Peerless, the Most Exalted. Unto Him have I resigned Myself and into His hands have I committed all My affairs. No God is there besides Him, the supreme Ruler, the resplendent Truth. Indeed all-sufficient is He for Me; independently of all things doth He suffice, while nothing in the heavens or in the earth but Him sufficeth. He, in very truth, is the Self-Subsisting, the Most Severe.

Praise be unto Him Who at this very moment perceiveth

in this remote prison the goal of My desire. He is the One Who beareth witness unto Me at all times and beholdeth Me ere the inception of 'after Ḥín'.[1]

Why didst thou pronounce judgement without remembering God, the All-Wise? How canst thou endure in the fire? Indeed, mighty and most severe is thy God.

Thou pridest thyself in the things thou dost possess, yet no believer in God and in His signs, nor any righteous man would ever deign to regard them. This mortal life is like unto the carcass of a dog, around which none would gather, nor would any partake thereof, except those who gainsay the life hereafter. Verily it is incumbent upon thee to become a true believer in God, the All-Possessing, the Almighty, and to turn away from the one who guideth thee into the torment of hell-fire.

I have been waiting a while that perchance thou wouldst take heed and be rightly guided. How canst thou answer God on the day which is near at hand—the day whereon witnesses will stand forth to testify in the presence of thy Lord, the Lord of all the worlds?

By the righteousness of Him Who hath called thee into being and unto Whom ere long thou shalt return, if thou remainest, at the moment of death, a disbeliever in the signs of thy Lord thou shalt surely enter the gates of hell, and none of the deeds thy hands have wrought will profit thee, nor shalt thou find a patron nor anyone to plead for thee. Fear thou God and pride not thyself on thine earthly possessions, inasmuch as what God doth possess is better for them that tread the path of righteousness.

Verily in this Day all that dwell on earth are the servants

[1] The numerical value of the letters of the word Ḥín is 68. The year 1268 A.H. (1851–1852 A.D.) is the year preceding the birth of the Baháʼí Revelation.

of God. As to those who truly believe in God and are well assured in the signs revealed by Him, perchance He will graciously forgive them the things their hands have committed, and will grant them admission into the precincts of His mercy. He, in truth, is the Ever-Forgiving, the Compassionate. But the verdict of divine chastisement is pronounced against those who have turned away disdainfully from Me and have repudiated the conclusive proofs and the unerring Book with which God hath invested Me, and on the Day of Severing they shall find no protector or helper.

I swear by Him Who createth all beings and unto Whom all shall return, if anyone at the hour of death beareth hatred towards Me or disputeth the clear tokens wherewith I have been invested, then naught but afflictive torment shall be his lot. On that day no ransom will be accepted, nor will any intercession be permitted, unless God so please. Verily He is the All-Compelling, the All-Glorious; and no God is there other than Him, the sovereign Ruler, the Almighty, the Most Severe.

If thou rejoicest in My imprisonment, woe then unto thee for the grievous torment which will soon overtake thee. Indeed God hath permitted no one to pass unfair judgement, and if thou wouldst fain do so, then soon shalt thou learn.

From the first day that I cautioned thee not to wax proud before God until the present time, four years have elapsed, and during this space naught have I witnessed, either from thee or from thy soldiers, except dire oppression and disdainful arrogance. Methinks thou dost imagine that I wish to gain some paltry substance from this earthly life. Nay, by the righteousness of My Lord! In the estimation of them that have fixed their eyes upon the merciful Lord, the riches of the world and its trappings are worth as much as the eye of a dead body, nay even less. Far from His glory be what they associate with Him! . . . I seek patience only in God. Verily He is the best protector and the best helper. No refuge do I seek save God. Verily He is the guardian and the best supporter . . .

I swear by the glory of God, My Lord, the Most Exalted, the Most Great, He assuredly, as is divinely ordained, will make His Cause shine resplendent, while there will be no helper for the unjust. If thou hast any scheme, produce thy scheme. Indeed every revelation of authority proceedeth from God. In Him do I trust and unto Him do I turn.

Hast thou heard anyone of old passing a judgement similar to the one thou didst contrive or like unto that whereto thou didst give thine assent? Woe then unto the oppressors! Both thine intentions and the manner in which thou dealest with the people clearly demonstrate thine infidelity towards God, hence He hath ordained a severe chastisement for thee. Verily I seek patience only in God, and Him do I regard as the goal of My desire. This signifieth that I have the undoubted Truth on My side.

If thou art not apprehensive that the truth might be revealed and the works of the ungodly be brought to naught, why summonest thou not the divines of the land, and then summon Me, so that I may confound them forthwith, even as those disbelievers whom I have previously confounded? This is My sure testimony unto thee and unto them, if they speak the truth. Summon thou all of them. Should they then be able to utter words like unto this, thou wouldst know that their cause is worthy of attention. Nay, by the righteousness of My Lord! They are bereft of power, nor are they endued with perception. They professed faith in the past without understanding its significance, then later they repudiated the Truth; for they are devoid of discernment.

If thou hast decided to shed My blood, wherefore dost thou delay? Thou art now endowed with power and authority. For Me it will prove an infinite bounty conferred by God, while for thee and for them that would commit such an act it will amount to a chastisement meted out by Him.

How great the blessedness that would await Me, wert thou to pass a verdict such as this; and what immense joy would be Mine, shouldst thou agree to do this! This is a bounty which God hath reserved for them that enjoy near access to His court. Give then thy leave and wait no longer. In truth, mighty is thy Lord, the Avenger.

Art thou not ashamed in the presence of God for consenting to the consignment to a fortress of Him Who is the Testimony of God, and His being made captive in the hands of the faithless? Woe betide thee and them who rejoice at this moment in inflicting so dire a humiliation upon Me . . .

I swear by Him Who hath called Me into being, I can discover no trace of sinfulness in Myself, nor have I followed aught but the Truth; and unto Me God is sufficient witness. Fie upon the world and its people and upon those who take delight in earthly riches, while oblivious of the life to come.

Were the veil to be removed from thine eye thou wouldst crawl unto Me on thy breast, even through the snow, from fear of the chastisement of God which is swift and near at hand. By the righteousness of Him Who hath created thee, wert thou to be acquainted with that which hath transpired during thy reign, thou wouldst wish not to have issued from thy father's loins, but rather to have passed into oblivion. However, that which God, thy Lord, had ordained hath presently come to pass, and woe betide the oppressors in this day.

Methinks thou hast not perused the unerring Book. If thou art satisfied with thine own way and dost not wish to follow the Truth, then to Me be My way and to thee thine. If thou aidest Me not, why dost thou seek to abase Me? Verily, God is the hearer of the suppliant, and in Him all things find their highest consummation, both in this world and in the world to come.

Far from the glory of God, the Lord of heaven and earth, the Lord of creation, be that which is affirmed of Him by the peoples of the world, except by such as faithfully observe His precepts. May the peace of God rest upon the sincere among His servants.

All praise be to God, the Lord of all the worlds.

EXTRACTS FROM A FURTHER EPISTLE TO
MUḤAMMAD SHÁH

THIS is an Epistle from Him Who is the true, the undoubted Leader. Herein is revealed the law of all things for
those who fain would heed His Call or wish to be reckoned
among them that are guided aright. Herein is enshrined the
law of all things for such as would bear witness to the
Revelation of thy Lord in accordance with this clear
balance. Verily the ordinances of God concerning all things
were formerly set forth in eloquent Arabic. Indeed those
whose souls have been created through the splendour of
the light of thy Lord recognize the Truth and are numbered
with such as faithfully obey the One True God and are well
assured . . .

O Muḥammad! The Decree of thy Lord was fulfilled
four years ago; and ever since the inception of the Cause
of thy Lord I have warned thee to fear God and not to be of
the ignorant. I despatched a messenger unto thee with a
truly resplendent Tablet, but the followers of the devil
turned him away disdainfully and interposed themselves
between him and thee. They expelled him from the land
whereof thou art the undisputed sovereign. Thus hath the
good of this world and of the next escaped thee, unless thou
submit to the commandment ordained by God and be of
them that are rightly guided.

On My return from the sacred House of God[1] I sent thee
a Message similar to, nay even greater than the one I had
previously sent unto thee. Indeed God is the best protector

[1] The Ka'bah in Mecca

and witness. I despatched a messenger unto thee with Epistles revealed by Me, that thou mightest obey the command of God and not be of them that have repudiated the Truth. The oppressor, however, committed a thing the like of which no one would commit, not even any of the wicked, nor anyone among the vile wrong-doers . . . The tribulations which I have suffered in this land, no one of old hath suffered. Verily unto God shall revert the whole affair, and He in truth is the best protector and is cognizant of all. The things which have, from the first day till now, befallen Me at the hand of thy people are but the work of Satan.[1] Ever since the Cause of thy Lord hath appeared none of thy deeds hath been acceptable, and thou hast been lost in palpable error while all thou couldst see appeared to thee as deeds performed for the sake of thy Lord. In truth thy day is nigh at hand and thou shalt be questioned concerning all this, and assuredly God is not heedless of the deeds of the wicked.

Had it not been for thee, thy supporters would not have disdainfully rejected Me, though they have gone more widely astray than the foolish.

Dost thou imagine him whom thou hast appointed Chancellor in thy kingdom to be the best leader and the best supporter? Nay, I swear by thy Lord. He will bring thee into grievous trouble by reason of that which Satan instilleth in his heart, and verily, he himself is Satan. He comprehendeth not a single letter from the Book of God and is seized with fear by reason of that which his hands have wrought. Fain would he extinguish the light which thy Lord hath kindled, so that the old impiety which is concealed in his inner being may not be revealed. Hadst thou not appointed him as thy Chancellor no one would

[1] cf. Qur'án 4:119

have paid him the slightest attention. Indeed in the estimation of the people he is naught but manifest darkness . . .

Fear thou God and suffer not thy soul to be chastised beyond that with which it hath already been tormented; for ere long thou shalt pass away and shalt declare thyself clear of the devil whom thou hast appointed as thy Chancellor, saying: 'O would that I had not taken the devil as my Chancellor, nor appointed an impostor as my guide and adviser.'

Why dost thou burden thy soul with that which is far more abject than the deeds of Pharaoh, and still callest thyself one of the faithful? How dost thou peruse the verses of the Qur'án, while thou art of the unjust? Never would the Jews, nor the Christians nor any such people as have rejected the truth consent to inflict wrongs upon the son of their Prophet's daughter. Woe betide thee, for the day of chastisement is approaching. Dost thou not dread the wrath of thy Lord, the Almighty, the Lord of the heavens, the Lord of all worlds? Indeed these manifest verses are conclusive testimony for those who seek true guidance.

I have no desire to seize thy property, even to the extent of a grain of mustard, nor do I wish to occupy thy position. If thou followest Me not, then unto thee be the things thou dost possess, and unto Me the land of unfailing security. If thou obeyest Me not, wherefore dost thou look disdainfully upon Me and seek to treat Me with sore injustice? Verily, behold My habitation—a lofty mountain wherein no one dwelleth. Woe betide them that wrongfully do injustice to people, and unjustly and deceitfully usurp the property of the believers in violation of His lucid Book; whereas I, Who, in very truth, am the rightful Sovereign of all men, designated by the true, the undeniable Leader, would never infringe on the integrity of the substance of the people, were it to the extent of a grain of mustard, nor would I treat them unjustly. Rather would I consort with them even as one of themselves, and I would be their witness. That which devolveth upon Me is but to mention the Book of thy Lord and to deliver this clear Message. If thou wishest to enter the gates of Paradise, lo, they are open before thy face and no harm can reach Me from anyone. Every missive which up till now I have directed unto thee and unto the custodian of thy affairs hath been but a token of My bounty to you both, that perchance ye may grow anxious about the day which is nigh at hand. Nevertheless from the moment ye waxed disdainful, divine judgement was passed upon you in the Book of God, for in truth ye both have denied your Lord and are numbered with them that will perish . . . This is indeed My last reminder unto you, and I shall make no mention of you hereafter, nor shall I make any remark other than affirming you as infidels.

Unto God do I commit Mine affair and yours, and He verily is the best Judge. Were ye to return, however, ye would be granted whatever ye desire of earthly possessions and of the ineffable delights of the life to come, and ye would inherit such glorious might and majesty as your minds can scarce conceive in this mortal life. But if ye fail to return then upon ye shall be your transgressions.

Ye cannot alter the things which the Almighty hath prescribed unto Me. Naught shall touch Me besides that which God, My Lord, hath pre-ordained for Me. In Him have I placed My whole trust and upon Him do the faithful place their complete reliance.

Bear Thou witness unto Me, O Lord. By sending forth this resplendent Epistle I shall have proclaimed Thy Verses unto both of them and shall have fulfilled Thy Testimony for them. I am well pleased to lay down My life in Thy path and ere long to return to Thy presence. Unto Thee be praise in the heavens and on the earth. Deal with them according to Thy decree. In truth Thou art the best protector and helper.

Set right, O Lord, such disorders as people stir up, and cause Thy Word to shine resplendent throughout the earth, so that no trace of the ungodly may remain.

I beg forgiveness of Thee, O My Lord, for that which I have uttered in Thy Epistle, and I repent unto Thee. I am but one of Thy servants who give praise to Thee. Glorified art Thou; no God is there but Thee. In Thee have I placed My whole trust and of Thee do I beg pardon for being a suppliant at Thy door.

Sanctified is God thy Lord, the Lord of the Mighty Throne, from that which the people wrongfully and without the guidance of His lucid Book, affirm of Him. Peace be upon them that beseech forgiveness from God thy Lord, saying: 'Verily, praise be unto God, the Lord of the worlds.'

O SHERIF! . . . All thy life thou hast accorded worship unto Us, but when We manifested Ourself unto thee, thou didst desist from bearing witness unto Our Remembrance, and from affirming that He is indeed the Most Exalted, the Sovereign Truth, the All-Glorious. Thus hath Thy Lord put thee to proof in the Day of Resurrection. Verily He is the All-Knowing, the All-Wise.

For hadst thou uttered 'Here am I' at the time We sent thee the Book, We would have admitted thee to the company of such of Our servants as truly believe, and would have graciously praised thee in Our Book, until the Day when all men shall appear before Us for judgement. This is in truth far more advantageous unto thee than all the acts of worship thou hast performed for thy Lord during all thy life, nay, from the beginning that hath no beginning. Assuredly this is what would have served and will ever serve thy best interests. Verily We are cognizant of all things. Yet notwithstanding that We had called thee into being for the purpose of attaining Our presence in the Day of Resurrection, thou didst shut thyself out from Us without any reason or explicit Writ; whereas hadst thou been among such as are endowed with the knowledge of the Bayán, thou wouldst have, at the sight of the Book, testified forthwith that there is no God but Him, the Help in Peril, the Self-Subsisting, and wouldst have affirmed that He Who hath revealed the Qur'án, hath likewise revealed this Book, that every word of it is from God, and unto it we all bear allegiance.

However, that which was preordained hath come to pass. Shouldst thou return unto Us while revelation still continueth through Us, We shall transform thy fire into light. Truly We are powerful over all things. But if thou failest in this task, thou shalt find no way open to thee other than to embrace the Cause of God and to implore that the matter of thine allegiance be brought to the attention of Him Whom God shall make manifest, that He may graciously enable thee to prosper and cause thy fire to be transformed into light. This is that which hath been sent down unto Us. Should this not come to pass, whatever We have set down shall remain binding and irrevocably decreed by God, the Help in Peril, the Self-Subsisting, and We shall therefore banish thee from Our presence as a token of justice on Our part. Verily we are equitable in Our judgement.

O 'ABDU'Ṣ-ṢÁḤIB! Verily God and every created thing testify that there is none other God but Me, the Almighty, the Best Beloved ... Thy vision is obscured by the belief that divine revelation ended with the coming of Muḥammad, and unto this We have borne witness in Our first epistle. Indeed, He Who hath revealed verses unto Muḥammad, the Apostle of God, hath likewise revealed verses unto 'Alí-Muḥammad. For who else but God can reveal to a man such clear and manifest verses as overpower all the learned? Since thou hast acknowledged the revelation of Muḥammad, the Apostle of God, then there is no other way open before thee but to testify that whatever is revealed by the Primal Point hath also proceeded from God, the Help in Peril, the Self-Subsisting. Is it not true that the Qur'án hath been sent down from God and that all men are powerless before its revelation? Likewise these words have also been revealed by God, if thou dost but perceive. What is there in the Bayán which keepeth thee back from recognizing these verses as being sent forth by God, the Inaccessible, the Most Exalted, the All-Glorious?

The essence of these words is this: Were We to bring thee to a reckoning, thou wouldst prove thyself empty-handed; We in truth know all things. Hadst thou uttered 'yea' on hearing the Words of God, thou wouldst have been seen to have been worshipping God from the beginning that hath no beginning until the present day, never to have disobeyed Him, not even for the twinkling of an eye.

Yet, neither the upright deeds thou hast wrought during all thy life, nor the exertions thou didst make to banish every thought from thy heart save that of the good-pleasure of God, none of these did in truth profit thee, not even to the extent of a grain of mustard seed, inasmuch as thou didst veil thyself from God and tarried behind at the time of His manifestation.

Verily all the divines in the land of Káf [Kúfih] shall, even as thyself, be asked by God: 'Is it not strange that a Messenger should have come to you with a Book, and ye, while confessing your powerlessness, refused to follow the Faith of God which He had brought, and ye persisted in your disbelief?' Therefore unto thee shall be assigned the fire which was meant for those who turned away from God in that land, inasmuch as thou art their leader; would that thou might be of them who heed.

Hadst thou faithfully obeyed the Decree of God, all the inhabitants of thy land would have followed thee, and would have themselves entered into the celestial Paradise, content with the good-pleasure of God for evermore. However, on that day thou shalt wish that God had not created thee.

Thou hast set thyself up as one of the learned in the Faith of Islám, that thou mightest save the believers, yet thou didst cause thy followers to descend into the fire, for when the verses of God were sent forth thou didst deprive thyself therefrom and yet reckoned thyself to be of the righteous . . . Nay, by the life of Him Whom God shall make manifest! Neither thou nor any one among His servants can produce the slightest proof, while God shineth resplendent above His creatures and through the power of His behest standeth supreme over all that dwell in the kingdoms of heaven and earth and in whatever lieth between them. Verily He is potent over all created things.

Thou hast named thyself 'Abdu'ṣ Ṣáḥib [servant of the Lord]. Yet, while God hath, in very truth, made thy Lord manifest, and thou didst set thine eyes upon Him, thou didst not recognize Him, even though thou hadst been called into being by God for the purpose of attaining His presence, didst thou but truly believe in the third verse of the chapter entitled 'Thunder'.[1]

Thou contendest, 'How can we recognize Him when we have heard naught but words which fall short of irrefutable proofs?' Yet since thou hast acknowledged and recognized Muḥammad, the Apostle of God, through the Qur'án, how canst thou withhold recognition from Him Who sent thee the Book, despite thy calling thyself 'His servant'? Verily He doth exercise undisputed authority over His revelations unto all mankind.

Wert thou to come unto Us while divine revelation is descending upon Us, haply God will change thy fire into light. Verily He is the Ever-Forgiving, the Most Generous. Otherwise that which hath been revealed is decisive and final and will be faithfully upheld by all until the Day of Resurrection ... If divine revelation ceaseth, thou shouldst write a petition to Him Whom God shall make manifest, imploring that it be delivered into His presence. Therein thou must beg pardon of thy Lord, turn unto Him in repentance and be of them that are wholly devoted to Him. Perchance God will transform thy fire into light at the next Resurrection. He, of a truth, is the Protector, the Most Exalted, the Ever-Forgiving. Unto Him bow down in worship all that are in the heavens and on the earth and whatever lieth between them; and unto Him shall all return.

We enjoin thee to save thyself and all the inhabitants of

[1] Qur'án 13

that land from the fire, then to enter the peerless and exalted Paradise of His good-pleasure. Otherwise the day is approaching when thou shalt perish and enter the fire, when thou shalt have neither patron nor helper from God. We have taken compassion on thee, as a sign of Our grace, inasmuch as thou hast related thyself unto Us. Verily We are aware of all things. We are cognizant of thy righteous deeds, though they shall avail thee nothing; for the whole object of such righteousness is but recognition of God, thy Lord, and undoubted faith in the Words revealed by Him.

ADDRESS TO SULAYMÁN, ONE OF THE MUSLIM
DIVINES IN THE LAND OF MASQAṬ

THIS is an Epistle from God, the Help in Peril, the Self-Subsisting, unto Sulaymán in the land of Masqaṭ, to the right of the Sea. In truth there is none other God but Him, the Help in Peril, the Self-Subsisting . . . Indeed, were all the inhabitants of heaven and earth and whatever existeth between them to assemble together, they would utterly fail and be powerless to produce such a book, even though We made them masters of eloquence and learning on earth. Since thou dost adduce proofs from the Qur'án, God shall, with proofs from that self-same Book, vindicate Himself in the Bayán. This is none other than a decree of God; He is truly the All-Knowing, the All-Powerful.

If thou art of them that truly believe, thou hast no other alternative than to bear allegiance unto it. This is the Way of God for all the inhabitants of earth and heaven and all that lieth betwixt them. No God is there but Me, the Almighty, the Inaccessible, the Most Exalted.

From this land We then proceeded to the sacred House, and on Our return journey We landed once again at this spot, when We perceived that thou hadst heeded not that which We sent thee, nor art thou of them that truly believe. Although We had created thee to behold Our countenance, and We did actually alight in thy locality, yet thou didst fail to attain the object of thy creation, and this despite thy worshipping God all thy life. Wherefore vain shall be the deeds thou hast wrought, by reason of thy being shut out as by a veil from Our presence and from Our Writings.

This is an irrevocable decree ordained by Us. Verily We are equitable in Our judgement.

Hadst thou observed the contents of the Epistle We sent unto thee, it would have been far more profitable to thee than worshipping thy Lord from the beginning that hath no beginning until this day, and indeed more meritorious than proving thyself wholly devoted in thine acts of worship. And hadst thou attained the presence of thy Lord in this land, and been of them that truly believe that the Face of God is beheld in the person of the Primal Point, it would have been far more advantageous than prostrating thyself in adoration from the beginning that hath no beginning until the present time. . . .

In truth We tested thee and found that thou wert not of them that are endowed with understanding, wherefore We passed upon thee the sentence of negation, as a token of justice from Our presence; and verily We are equitable.

However, shouldst thou return unto Us, We would convert thy negation into affirmation. Verily We are the One Who is of immense bounteousness. But should the Primal Point cease to be with you, then the judgement given in the Words of God shall be final and unalterable and every one will assuredly uphold it.

Wert thou to address a letter to Him Whom God shall make manifest, begging that it be delivered unto His presence, perchance He would graciously forgive thee and, at His behest, turn thy negation into affirmation. He is in truth the All-Bountiful, the Most Generous, He Whose grace is infinite. Otherwise, no way shalt thou find open unto thee and no benefit shalt thou gain from the deeds thou hast wrought, by reason of thy failure to respond 'yea, here am I'. Verily We have reduced thee and thy works to naught, as though thou hadst never come into existence nor ever been of them that do good works, that this may serve as a lesson for those unto whom the Bayán is given, that they may take good heed when the sacred Writings of Him Whom God shall make manifest will reach them and perchance, by pondering upon them, may be enabled to save their own souls.

Our grace assuredly pervadeth all that dwell in the kingdoms of earth and heaven and in whatever lieth between them, and beyond them all mankind. However, souls that have shut themselves out as by a veil can never partake of the outpourings of the grace of God.

2

EXCERPTS FROM THE QAYYÚMU'L-ASMÁ'

LL praise be to God Who hath, through the power of Truth, sent down this Book unto His servant, that it may serve as a shining light for all mankind . . . Verily this is none other than the sovereign Truth; it is the Path which God hath laid out for all that are in heaven and on earth. Let him then who will, take for himself the right path unto his Lord. Verily this is the true Faith of God, and sufficient witness are God and such as are endowed with the knowledge of the Book. This is indeed the eternal Truth which God, the Ancient of Days, hath revealed unto His omnipotent Word—He Who hath been raised up from the midst of the Burning Bush. This is the Mystery which hath been hidden from all that are in heaven and on earth, and in this wondrous Revelation it hath, in very truth, been set forth in the Mother Book by the hand of God, the Exalted . . .

O concourse of kings and of the sons of kings! Lay aside, one and all, your dominion which belongeth unto God . . .

Let not thy sovereignty deceive thee, O Sháh, for 'every soul shall taste of death,'[1] and this, in very truth, hath been written down as a decree of God. *Chapter I.*

O King of Islám! Aid thou, with the truth, after having aided the Book, Him Who is Our Most Great Remembrance, for God hath, in very truth, destined for thee, and for such as circle round thee, on the Day of Judgement, a responsible position in His Path. I swear by God, O Sháh!

[1] Qur'án 3:182

If thou showest enmity unto Him Who is His Remembrance, God will, on the Day of Resurrection, condemn thee, before the kings, unto hell-fire, and thou shalt not, in very truth, find on that Day any helper except God, the Exalted. Purge thou, O S͟háh, the Sacred Land [Ṭihrán] from such as have repudiated the Book, ere the day whereon the Remembrance of God cometh, terribly and of a sudden, with His potent Cause, by the leave of God, the Most High. God, verily, hath prescribed to thee to submit unto Him Who is His Remembrance, and unto His Cause, and to subdue, with the truth and by His leave, the countries, for in this world thou hast been mercifully invested with sovereignty, and wilt, in the next, dwell, nigh unto the Seat of Holiness, with the inmates of the Paradise of His good-pleasure . . .

By God! If ye do well, to your own behoof will ye do well; and if ye deny God and His signs, We, in very truth, having God, can well dispense with all creatures and all earthly dominion. *Chapter I.*

BE thou content with the commandment of God, the True One, inasmuch as sovereignty, as recorded in the Mother Book by the hand of God, is surely invested in Him Who is His Remembrance . . .

O Minister of the S͟háh! Fear thou God, besides Whom there is none other God but Him, the Sovereign Truth, the Just, and lay aside thy dominion, for We, by the leave of God, the All-Wise, inherit the earth and all who are upon it,[1] and He shall rightfully be a witness unto thee and unto

[1] cf. Qur'án 19:41

the S͟háh. Were ye to obey the Remembrance of God with absolute sincerity, We guarantee, by the leave of God, that on the Day of Resurrection, a vast dominion shall be yours in His eternal Paradise.

Vain indeed is your dominion, for God hath set aside earthly possessions for such as have denied Him; for unto Him Who is your Lord shall be the most excellent abode, He Who is, in truth, the Ancient of Days. ...

O concourse of kings! Deliver with truth and in all haste the verses sent down by Us to the peoples of Turkey and of India, and beyond them, with power and with truth, to lands in both the East and the West. ... And know that if ye aid God, He will, on the Day of Resurrection, graciously aid you, upon the Bridge, through Him Who is His Most Great Remembrance ...

O people of the earth! Whoso obeyeth the Remembrance of God and His Book hath in truth obeyed God and His chosen ones and he will, in the life to come, be reckoned in the presence of God among the inmates of the Paradise of His good-pleasure. *Chapter I.*

VERILY We made the revelation of verses to be a testimony for Our message unto you. Can ye produce a single letter to match these verses? Bring forth, then, your proofs, if ye be of those who can discern the one true God. I solemnly affirm before God, should all men and spirits combine to compose the like of one chapter of this Book, they would surely fail, even though they were to assist one another.[1]

[1] cf. Qur'án 17:90

O concourse of divines! Fear God from this day onwards in the views ye advance, for He Who is Our Remembrance in your midst, and Who cometh from Us, is, in very truth, the Judge and Witness. Turn away from that which ye lay hold of, and which the Book of God, the True One, hath not sanctioned, for on the Day of Resurrection ye shall, upon the Bridge, be, in very truth, held answerable for the position ye occupied. . . . And unto you We have sent down this Book which truly none can mistake . . .

O concourse of the people of the Book! Fear ye God and pride not yourselves in your learning. Follow ye the Book which His Remembrance hath revealed in praise of God, the True One. He Who is the Eternal Truth beareth me witness, whoso followeth this Book hath indeed followed all the past Scriptures which have been sent down from heaven by God, the Sovereign Truth. Verily, He is well informed of what ye do . . . Such as are the true followers of Islám would say: 'O Lord our God! We have hearkened to the call of Thy Remembrance and obeyed Him. Forgive us our sins. Thou art, verily, the Eternal Truth, and unto Thee, our infallible Retreat, must we all return.'[1] *Chapter II.*

As to those who deny Him Who is the Sublime Gate of God, for them We have prepared, as justly decreed by God, a sore torment. And He, God, is the Mighty, the Wise.

We have, of a truth, sent down this divinely-inspired Book unto Our Servant . . . Ask ye then Him Who is Our Remembrance of its interpretation, inasmuch as He, as

[1] cf. Qur'án 2:285

divinely-ordained and through the grace of God, is invested with the knowledge of its verses . . .

O children of men! If ye believe in the one True God, follow Me, this Most Great Remembrance of God sent forth by your Lord, that He may graciously forgive you your sins. Verily He is forgiving and compassionate toward the concourse of the faithful. We, of a truth, choose the Messengers through the potency of Our Word, and We exalt Their offspring, some over others, through the Great Remembrance of God as decreed in the Book and concealed therein . . .

Some of the people of the city have declared: 'We are the helpers of God', but when this Remembrance came suddenly upon them, they turned aside from helping Us. Verily God is My Lord and your true Lord, therefore worship Him, while this Path from 'Alí [the Báb] is none but the straight Path[1] in the estimation of your Lord. *Chapter III.*

UNTO every people We have sent down the Book in their own language.[2] This Book We have, verily, revealed in the language of Our Remembrance and it is in truth a wondrous language. He is, verily, the eternal Truth come from God, and according to the divine judgement given in the Mother Book, He is the most distinguished among the writers of Arabic and most eloquent in His utterance. He is in truth the Supreme Talisman and is endowed with supernatural powers, as set forth in the Mother Book . . .

[1] cf. Qur'án 3:50
[2] cf. ibid. 14:4

O people of the city! Ye have disbelieved your Lord. If ye are truly faithful to Muḥammad, the Apostle of God and the Seal of the Prophets, and if ye follow His Book, the Qur'án, which is free from error, then here is the like of it—this Book, which We have, in truth and by the leave of God, sent down unto Our Servant. If ye fail to believe in Him, then your faith in Muḥammad and His Book which was revealed in the past will indeed be treated as false in the estimation of God. If ye deny Him, the fact of your having denied Muḥammad and His Book will, in very truth and with absolute certainty, become evident unto yourselves. *Chapter IV.*

Fear ye God and breathe not a word concerning His Most Great Remembrance other than what hath been ordained by God, inasmuch as We have established a separate covenant regarding Him with every Prophet and His followers. Indeed, We have not sent any Messenger without this binding covenant and We do not, of a truth, pass judgement upon anything except after the covenant of Him Who is the Supreme Gate hath been established. Ere long the veil shall be lifted from your eyes at the appointed time. Ye shall then behold the sublime Remembrance of God, unclouded and vivid. *Chapter V.*

Do men imagine that We are far distant from the people of the world? Nay, the day We cause them to be assailed by the pangs of death[1] they shall, upon the plain of Resurrection, behold how the Lord of Mercy and His Remembrance were near. Thereupon they shall exclaim: 'Would that we had followed the path of the Báb! Would that we had sought refuge only with Him, and not with men of perversity and error! For verily the Remembrance of God appeared before us,[2] behind us, and on all sides, yet we were, in very truth, shut out as by a veil from Him.' *Chapter VII.*

Do not say, 'How can He speak of God while in truth His age is no more than twenty-five?' Give ye ear unto Me. I swear by the Lord of the heavens and of the earth: I am verily a servant of God. I have been made the Bearer of irrefutable proofs from the presence of Him Who is the long-expected Remnant of God. Here is My Book before your eyes, as indeed inscribed in the presence of God in the Mother Book. God hath indeed made Me blessed, wheresoever I may be, and hath enjoined upon Me to observe prayer and fortitude so long as I shall live on earth amongst you. *Chapter IX.*

Glorified is He besides Whom there is none other God. In His grasp He holdeth the source of authority, and verily God is powerful over all things. We have decreed

[1] cf. Qur'án 68:42
[2] cf. ibid. 7:63, 69

that every long life shall in truth suffer decline[1] and that every hardship shall be followed by ease,[2] that perchance men may recognise the Gate of God as He Who is the eternal Truth, and verily God shall stand as witness unto those that have believed. *Chapter XIII.*

O YE servants of God! Verily, be not grieved if a thing ye asked of Him remaineth unanswered, inasmuch as He hath been commanded by God to observe silence, a silence which is in truth praiseworthy. We have indeed enabled Thee to truly see in Thy dream a measure of Our Cause, but wert Thou to acquaint them with the hidden Mystery, they would dispute its truth among themselves. Verily Thy Lord, the God of truth, knoweth the very secrets of hearts[3] ...

O peoples of the world! Whatsoever ye have offered up in the way of the One True God, ye shall indeed find preserved by God, the Preserver, intact at God's Holy Gate. O peoples of the earth! Bear ye allegiance unto this resplendent light wherewith God hath graciously invested Me through the power of infallible Truth, and walk not in the footsteps of the Evil One,[4] inasmuch as he prompteth you to disbelieve in God, your Lord, and verily God will not forgive disbelief in Himself, though He will forgive other sins to whomsoever He pleaseth.[5] Indeed His knowledge embraceth all things ... *Chapter XVII.*

[1] cf. Qur'án 36:68
[2] cf. ibid. 65:7; 94:5
[3] cf. ibid. 8:45
[4] cf. ibid. 2:204
[5] cf. ibid. 4:51

O PEOPLES of the East and the West! Be ye fearful of God concerning the Cause of the true Joseph and barter Him not for a paltry price[1] established by yourselves, or for a trifle of your earthly possessions, that ye may, in very truth, be praised by Him as those who are reckoned among the pious who stand nigh unto this Gate. Verily God hath deprived of His grace him who martyred Ḥusayn, Our forefather, lonely and forsaken as He was upon the land of Ṭaff [Karbilá]. Yazíd, the son of Muʻávíyih, out of corrupt desire, bartered away the head of the true Joseph to the fiendish people for a trifling price and a petty sum from his property. Verily they repudiated God by committing a grievous error. Erelong will God wreak His vengeance upon them, at the time of Our Return, and He hath, in very truth, prepared for them, in the world to come, a severe torment. *Chapter XXI.*

O QURRATU'L-ʻAYN![2] We have, verily, dilated Thine heart in this Revelation, which stands truly unique from all created things, and have exalted Thy name through the manifestation of the Báb, so that men may become aware of Our transcendent power, and recognize that God is immeasurably sanctified above the praise of all men. He is verily independent of the whole of creation. *Chapter XXIII.*

[1] cf. Qur'án 12:20
[2] In these passages of the Qayyúmu'l-Asmá' the name Qurratu'l-ʻAyn (Solace of the Eyes) refers to the Báb Himself.

THE angels and the spirits, arrayed rank upon rank, descend, by the leave of God, upon this Gate[1] and circle round this Focal Point in a far-stretching line. Greet them with salutations, O Qurratu'l-'Ayn, for the dawn hath indeed broken; then proclaim unto the concourse of the faithful: 'Is not the rising of the Morn, foreshadowed in the Mother Book, to be near at hand?[2] . . .'

O Qurratu'l-'Ayn! Turn Thou eagerly unto God in Thy Cause, for the peoples of the world have risen in iniquity, and but for the outpouring of the grace of God and Thy mercy unto them, no one could purge even a single soul for evermore.[3] O Qurratu'l-'Ayn! The life to come is indeed far more advantageous unto Thee and unto such as follow Thy Cause than this earthly life and its pleasures. This is what hath been foreordained according to the dispensations of Providence . . .

O Qurratu'l-'Ayn! Say: Verily I am the 'Gate of God' and I give you to drink, by the leave of God, the sovereign Truth, of the crystal-pure waters of His Revelation which are gushing out from the incorruptible Fountain situate upon the Holy Mount. And those who earnestly strive after the One True God, let them then strive to attain this Gate.[4] Verily God is potent over all things . . .

O peoples of the earth! Give ear unto God's holy Voice proclaimed by this Arabian Youth Whom the Almighty hath graciously chosen for His Own Self. He is indeed none other than the True One, Whom God hath entrusted with this Mission from the midst of the Burning Bush. O Qurratu'l-'Ayn! Unravel what Thou pleasest from the

[1] cf. Qur'án 78:38
[2] cf. ibid. 11:83
[3] cf. ibid. 24:21
[4] cf. ibid. 83:25–26

secrets of the All-Glorious, for the ocean is surging high[1] at the behest of the incomparable Lord. *Chapter XXIV.*

ARE ye wickedly scheming, according to your selfish fancies, an evil plot against Him Who is the Most Great Remembrance of God? By the righteousness of God, all who are in the heaven and on earth and whatsoever lieth between them are regarded in My sight even as a spider's web,[2] and verily God beareth witness unto all things. Indeed they will not lay plots but against themselves. God hath caused this Remembrance to be, in very truth, independent of all the dwellers of earth and heaven. *Chapter XXV.*

O YE peoples of the earth! During the time of My absence I sent down the Gates unto you. However the believers, except for a handful, obeyed them not. Formerly I sent forth unto you Aḥmad and more recently Kázim, but apart from the pure in heart amongst you no one followed them. What hath befallen you, O people of the Book? Will ye not fear the One true God, He Who is your Lord, the Ancient of Days? . . . O ye who profess belief in God! I adjure you by Him Who is the Eternal Truth, have ye discerned among the precepts of these Gates anything inconsistent with the commandments of God as set forth

1 Qur'án 52:6
2 cf. ibid. 29:40

in this Book? Hath your learning deluded you by reason of your impiety? Take ye heed then, for verily your God, the Lord of Eternal Truth, is with you and in very truth is watchful over you . . . *Chapter XXVII.*

O YE kinsmen of the Most Great Remembrance! This Tree of Holiness, dyed crimson with the oil of servitude, hath verily sprung forth out of your own soil in the midst of the Burning Bush, yet ye comprehend nothing whatever thereof, neither of His true, heavenly attributes, nor of the actual circumstances of His earthly life, nor of the evidences of His powerful and unblemished behaviour. Actuated by your own fancies, you consider Him to be alien to the sovereign Truth, while in the estimation of God He is none other than the Promised One Himself, invested with the power of the sovereign Truth, and verily He is, as decreed in the Mother Book, held answerable in the midst of the Burning Bush . . .

O Qurratu'l-'Ayn! Deliver the summons of the most exalted Word unto the handmaids among Thy kindred, caution them against the Most Great Fire and announce unto them the joyful tidings that following this mighty Covenant there shall be everlasting reunion with God in the Paradise of His good-pleasure, nigh unto the Seat of Holiness. Verily God, the Lord of creation, is potent over all things.

O Thou Mother of the Remembrance! May the peace and salutation of God rest upon thee. Indeed thou hast endured patiently in Him Who is the sublime Self of God. Recognize then the station of thy Son Who is none other than the mighty Word of God. He hath verily pledged Himself to be answerable for thee both in thy grave and on the Judgement Day, while thou hast, in the Preserved Tablet of God, been immortalized as the 'Mother of the Faithful' by the Pen of His Remembrance. *Chapter XXVIII.*

O QURRATU'L-'AYN! Stretch not Thy hands wide open in the Cause, inasmuch as the people would find themselves in a state of stupor by reason of the Mystery, and I swear by the true, Almighty God that there is yet for Thee another turn after this Dispensation.

And when the appointed hour hath struck, do Thou, by the leave of God, the All-Wise, reveal from the heights of the Most Lofty and Mystic Mount a faint, an infinitesimal glimmer of Thy impenetrable Mystery, that they who have recognized the radiance of the Sinaic Splendour may faint away and die as they catch a lightning glimpse of the fierce and crimson Light that envelops Thy Revelation. And God is, in very truth, Thine unfailing Protector. *Chapter XXVIII.*

O PEOPLE of Persia! Are ye not satisfied with this glorious honour which the supreme Remembrance of God hath conferred upon you? Verily ye have been especially favoured by God through this mighty Word. Then do not withdraw from the sanctuary of His presence, for, by the righteousness of the One true God, He is none other than the sovereign Truth from God; He is the most exalted One and the Source of all wisdom, as decreed in the Mother Book...

O peoples of the earth! Cleave ye tenaciously to the Cord of the All-Highest God, which is but this Arabian Youth, Our Remembrance—He Who standeth concealed at the point of ice amidst the ocean of fire. *Chapter XXIX.*

O PEOPLE of the earth! By the righteousness of the One true God, I am the Maid of Heaven begotten by the Spirit of Bahá, abiding within the Mansion hewn out of a mass of ruby, tender and vibrant; and in this mighty Paradise naught have I ever witnessed save that which proclaimeth the Remembrance of God by extolling the virtues of this Arabian Youth. Verily there is none other God but your Lord, the All-Merciful. Magnify ye, then, His station, for behold, He is poised in the midmost heart of the All-Highest Paradise as the embodiment of the praise of God in the Tabernacle wherein His glorification is intoned.

At one time I hear His Voice as He acclaimeth Him Who is the Ever-Living, the Ancient of Days, and at another time as He speaketh of the mystery of His most august Name. And when He intoneth the anthems of the greatness of God all Paradise waileth in its longing to gaze on His Beauty, and when He chanteth words of praise and glorification of God all Paradise becomes motionless like unto ice locked in the heart of a frost-bound mountain. Methinks I visioned Him moving along a straight middle path wherein every paradise was His Own paradise, every heaven His Own heaven, while the whole earth and all that is therein appeared but as a ring upon the finger of His

servants. Glorified be God, His Creator, the Lord of everlasting sovereignty. Verily He is none other but the servant
of God, the Gate of the Remnant of God your Lord, the
Sovereign Truth. *Chapter XXIX.*

O THOU the Supreme Word of God! Fear not, nor be
Thou grieved, for indeed unto such as have responded to
Thy Call, whether men or women, We have assured for-
giveness of sins, as known in the presence of the Best
Beloved and in conformity with what Thou desirest. Verily
His knowledge embraceth all things. I adjure Thee by My
life, set Thy face towards Me and be not apprehensive.
Verily Thou art the Exalted One among the Celestial Concourse, and Thy hidden Mystery hath, of a truth, been
recorded upon the Tablet of creation in the midst of the
Burning Bush. Ere long God will bestow upon Thee ruler-
ship over all men, inasmuch as His rule transcendeth the
whole of creation. *Chapter XXXI.*

O CONCOURSE of Shí'ihs! Fear ye God and Our Cause
which concerneth Him Who is the Most Great Remembrance of God. For great is its fire, as decreed in the Mother
Book. *Chapter XL.*

RECITE ye as much as convenient from this Qur'án both

at morn and at eventide, and chant the verses of this Book, by the leave of the eternal God, in the sweet accents of this Bird which warbleth its melody in the vault of heaven. *Chapter XLI.*

Issue forth from your cities, O peoples of the West and aid God ere the Day when the Lord of mercy shall come down unto you in the shadow of the clouds with the angels circling around Him,[1] exalting His praise and seeking forgiveness for such as have truly believed in Our signs. Verily His decree hath been issued, and the command of God, as given in the Mother Book, hath indeed been revealed ...

Become as true brethren in the one and indivisible religion of God, free from distinction, for verily God desireth that your hearts should become mirrors unto your brethren in the Faith, so that ye find yourselves reflected in them, and they in you. This is the true Path of God, the Almighty, and He is indeed watchful over your actions. *Chapter XLVI.*

O ye peoples of the earth! Hearken unto My call, ringing forth from the precincts of this sacred Tree—a Tree set ablaze by the pre-existent Fire: There is no God but Him; He is the Exalted, the All-Wise. O ye the servants of the Merciful One! Enter ye, one and all, through this Gate and

[1] cf. Qur'án 2:206

follow not the steps of the Evil One, for he prompteth you to walk in the ways of impiety and wickedness; he is, in truth, your declared enemy.[1] *Chapter LI.*

BE Thou patient, O Qurratu'l-'Ayn, for God hath indeed pledged to establish Thy sovereignty throughout all countries and over the people that dwell therein. He is God and verily He is powerful over all things. *Chapter LIII.*

BY My glory! I will make the infidels to taste, with the hands of My power, retributions unknown of any one except Me, and will waft over the faithful those musk-scented breaths which I have nursed in the midmost heart of My throne; and verily the knowledge of God embraceth all things.

O concourse of light! By the righteousness of God, We speak not according to selfish desire, nor hath a single letter of this Book been revealed save by the leave of God, the Sovereign Truth. Fear ye God and entertain no doubts regarding His Cause, for verily, the Mystery of this Gate is shrouded in the mystic utterances of His Writ and hath been written beyond the impenetrable veil of concealment by the hand of God, the Lord of the visible and the invisible.

Indeed God hath created everywhere around this Gate oceans of divine elixir, tinged crimson with the essence of existence and vitalized through the animating power of the

[1] cf. Qur'án 2:163-164

desired fruit; and for them God hath provided Arks of ruby, tender, crimson-coloured, wherein none shall sail but the people of Bahá, by the leave of God, the Most Exalted; and verily He is the All-Glorious, the All-Wise. *Chapter LVII.*

T HE Lord hath, in truth, inspired Me: Verily, verily, I am God, He besides Whom there is none other God, and I am indeed the Ancient of Days . . .

O people of the Kingdom! By the righteousness of the true God, if ye remain steadfast upon this line which standeth upright between the two lines, ye shall, in very truth, quaff the living waters from the Fountain of this wondrous Revelation as proffered by the hand of His Remembrance . . .

I swear by your true Lord, by Him Who is the Lord of the heavens and of the earth, that the divine Promise concerning His Remembrance is naught but the sovereign truth and, as decreed in the Mother Book, it shall come to pass . . .

Say, O peoples of the earth! Were ye to assemble together in order to produce the like of a single letter of My Works, ye would never be able to do so,[1] and verily God is cognizant of all things . . .

O Qurratu'l-'Ayn! Say: Behold! Verily the Moon hath faded; verily the night hath retreated; verily the dawn hath brightened;[2] verily the command of God, your true Lord, hath been accomplished . . .

[1] cf. Qur'án 17:88
[2] cf. ibid. 74:35–37

Out of utter nothingness, O great and omnipotent Master, Thou hast, through the celestial potency of Thy might, brought me forth and raised me up to proclaim this Revelation. I have made none other but Thee my trust; I have clung to no will but Thy Will. Thou art, in truth, the All-Sufficing and behind Thee standeth the true God, He Who overshadoweth all things. Indeed sufficient unto Me is God, the Exalted, the Powerful, the Sustainer. *Chapter LVIII.*

O THOU Remnant of God! I have sacrificed myself wholly for Thee; I have accepted curses for Thy sake, and have yearned for naught but martyrdom in the path of Thy love. Sufficient witness unto me is God, the Exalted, the Protector, the Ancient of Days.

O Qurratu'l-'Ayn! The words Thou hast uttered in this momentous Call have grieved Me bitterly. However, the irrevocable decision resteth with none but God and the decree proceedeth from none save Him alone. By My life, Thou art the Well-Beloved in the sight of God and His creation. Verily, there is no power except in God, and sufficient witness unto Me is your Lord, Who is, in very truth, the Omnipotent Avenger. *Chapter LVIII.*

O PEOPLES of the earth! By the righteousness of God, this Book hath, through the potency of the sovereign Truth, pervaded the earth and the heaven with the mighty Word of God concerning Him Who is the supreme Testimony, the Expected Qá'im, and verily God hath knowledge of all things. This divinely-inspired Book hath firmly established His Proof for all those who are in the East and in the West, hence beware lest ye utter aught but the truth regarding God, for I swear by your Lord that this supreme Proof of Mine beareth witness unto all things . . .

O servants of God! Be ye patient, for, God grant, He Who is the sovereign Truth will suddenly appear amongst you, invested with the power of the mighty Word, and ye shall then be confounded by the Truth itself, and ye shall have no power to ward it off;[1] and verily I am a witness over all mankind. *Chapter LIX.*

VERILY such as ridicule the wondrous, divine Verses revealed through His Remembrance, are but making themselves the objects of ridicule, and We, in truth, aid them to wax in their iniquity.[2] Indeed God's knowledge transcendeth all created things . . .

The infidels, of a truth, seek to separate God from His Remembrance,[3] but God hath determined to perfect His Light[4] through His Remembrance, and indeed He is potent over all things . . .

Verily, Christ is Our Word which We communicated unto Mary;[5] and let no one say what the Christians term

[1] cf. Qur'án 21:40
[2] cf. ibid. 2:14
[3] cf. ibid. 4:149
[4] cf. ibid. 9:32
[5] cf. ibid. 4:169

as 'the third of three',[1] inasmuch as it would amount to slandering the Remembrance Who, as decreed in the Mother Book, is invested with supreme authority. Indeed God is but one God, and far be it from His glory that there should be aught else besides Him. All those who shall attain unto Him on the Day of Resurrection are but His servants, and God is, of a truth, a sufficient Protector. Verily I am none other but the servant of God and His Word, and none but the first one to bow down in supplication before God, the Most Exalted; and indeed God witnesseth all things. *Chapter LXI.*

O PEOPLE of the Qur'án! Ye are as nothing unless ye submit unto the Remembrance of God and unto this Book. If ye follow the Cause of God, We will forgive you your sins, and if ye turn aside from Our command, We will, in truth, condemn your souls in Our Book, unto the Most Great Fire. We, verily, do not deal unjustly with men, even to the extent of a speck on a date-stone. *Chapter LXII.*

O PEOPLES of the earth! Verily the resplendent Light of God hath appeared in your midst, invested with this unerring Book, that ye may be guided aright to the ways of peace and, by the leave of God, step out of the darkness into the light and onto this far-extended Path of Truth[2] . . .

[1] Qur'án 5:77
[2] cf. ibid. 5:15–18

God hath out of sheer nothingness and through the potency of His command, created the heavens and the earth and whatever lieth between them. He is single and peerless in His eternal unity with none to join partner with His holy Essence, nor is there any soul, except His Own Self, who can befittingly comprehend Him . . .

O peoples of the earth! Verily His Remembrance is come to you from God after an interval during which there were no Messengers,[1] that He may purge and purify you from uncleanliness in anticipation of the Day of the One true God; therefore seek ye whole-heartedly divine blessings from Him, inasmuch as We have, in truth, chosen Him to be the Witness and the Source of wisdom unto all that dwell on earth . . .

O Qurratu'l-'Ayn! Proclaim that which hath been sent down unto Thee as a token of the grace of the merciful Lord, for if Thou do it not, Our secret will never be made known to the people,[2] while the purpose of God in creating man is but for him to know Him. Indeed God hath knowledge of all things and is self-sufficient above the need of all mankind. *Chapter LXII.*

WHENEVER the faithful hear the verses of this Book being recited, their eyes will overflow with tears and their hearts will be deeply touched by Him Who is the Most Great Remembrance for the love they cherish for God, the All-Praised. He is God, the All-Knowing, the Eternal. They are indeed the inmates of the all-highest Paradise wherein

[1] cf. Qur'án 5:22
[2] cf. ibid. 5:71

they will abide for ever. Verily they will see naught therein save that which hath proceeded from God, nothing that will lie beyond the compass of their understanding. There they will meet the believers in Paradise, who will address them with the words 'Peace, Peace' lingering on their lips ...

O concourse of the faithful! Incline your ears to My Voice, proclaimed by this Remembrance of God. Verily God hath revealed unto Me that the Path of the Remembrance which is set forth by Me is, in very truth, the straight Path of God, and that whoever professeth any religion other than this upright Faith, will, when called to account on the Day of Judgement, discover that as recorded in the Book no benefit hath he reaped out of God's Religion ...

Fear ye God, O concourse of kings, lest ye remain afar from Him Who is His Remembrance [the Báb], after the Truth hath come unto you with a Book and signs from God, as spoken through the wondrous tongue of Him Who is His Remembrance. Seek ye grace from God, for God hath ordained for you, after ye have believed in Him, a Garden the vastness of which is as the vastness of the whole of Paradise. Therein ye shall find naught save the gifts and favours which the Almighty hath graciously bestowed by virtue of this momentous Cause, as decreed in the Mother Book. *Chapter LXIII.*

O SPIRIT of God! Call Thou to mind the bounty which I bestowed upon Thee when I conversed with Thee in the midmost heart of My Sanctuary and aided Thee through the potency of the Holy Spirit that Thou mightest, as the peerless Mouthpiece of God, proclaim unto men the commandments of God which lie enshrined within the divine Spirit.

Verily God hath inspired Thee with divine verses and wisdom while still a child and hath graciously deigned to bestow His favour upon the peoples of the world through the influence of Thy Most Great Name, for indeed men have not the least knowledge of the Book. *Chapter LXIII.*

O PEOPLE of the earth! To attain the ultimate retreat in God, the True One, are we to seek a Gate other than this exalted Being? ...

When God created the Remembrance He presented Him to the assemblage of all created beings upon the altar of His Will. Thereupon the concourse of the angels bowed low in adoration to God, the Peerless, the Incomparable; while Satan waxed proud, refusing to submit to His Remembrance; hence he is identified in the Book of God as the arrogant one and the accursed.[1] *Chapter LXVII.*

GOD, besides Whom there is none other true God, saith: Indeed, whoso visiteth the Remembrance of God after His passing, it is as though he hath attained the presence of the Lord, seated upon His mighty Throne. Verily this is the Way of God, the Most Exalted, which hath been irrevocably decreed in the Mother Book ...

[1] cf. Qur'án 2:32; 38:74–78

Say, O peoples of the world! Do ye dispute with Me about God by virtue of the names which ye and your fathers have adopted for Him at the promptings of the Evil One?[1] God hath indeed sent down this Book unto Me with truth that ye may be enabled to recognize the true names of God, inasmuch as ye have strayed in error far from the Truth. Verily We have taken a covenant from every created thing upon its coming into being concerning the Remembrance of God, and there shall be none to avert the binding command of God for the purification of mankind, as ordained in the Book which is written by the hand of the Báb. *Chapter LXVIII.*

THE people, during the absence of the Báb, re-enacted the episode of the Calf by setting up a blaring figure which embodied animal features in human form[2] . . .

Whenever the people ask Thee of the appointed Hour say: Verily the knowledge of it is only with My Lord,[3] Who is the Knower of the unseen. There is none other God but Him—He Who hath created you from a single soul,[4] and I have no control over what profiteth Me or harmeth Me, but as My Lord pleaseth.[5] Indeed God is Self-Sufficient and He, My Lord, standeth supreme over all things. *Chapter LXIX.*

[1] cf. Qur'án 7:69; 12:40
[2] cf. ibid. 7:146; 20:90
[3] cf. ibid. 7:186
[4] cf. ibid. 4:1
[5] cf. ibid. 10:50

Doth it seem strange to the people that We should have revealed the Book to a man from among themselves in order to purge them and give them the good tidings that they shall be rewarded with a sure stance in the presence of their Lord? He indeed beareth witness unto all things ...

When the verses of this Book are recited to the infidels they say: 'Give us a book like the Qur'án and make changes in the verses.' Say: 'God hath not given Me that I should change them at My pleasure.' I follow only what is revealed unto Me. Verily, I shall fear My Lord on the Day of Separation, whose advent He hath, in very truth, irrevocably ordained.[1] *Chapter LXXI.*

O peoples of the earth! Verily the true God calleth saying: He Who is the Remembrance is indeed the sovereign Truth from God, and naught remaineth beyond truth but error,[2] and naught is there beyond error save fire, irrevocably ordained ...

O Qurratu'l-'Ayn! Point to Thy truthful breast through the power of truth and exclaim: I swear by the One true God, herein lieth the vicegerency of God; I am indeed the One Who is regarded as the Best Reward[3] and I am indeed He Who is the Most Excellent Abode. *Chapter LXXII.*

[1] cf. Qur'án 10:16
[2] cf. ibid. 10:33
[3] cf. ibid. 18:42

O YE concourse of the believers! Utter not words of denial against Me once the Truth is made manifest, for indeed the mandate of the Báb hath befittingly been proclaimed unto you in the Qur'án aforetime. I swear by your Lord, this Book is verily the same Qur'án which was sent down in the past. *Chapter LXXXI.*

O THOU cherished Fruit of the heart! Give ear to the melodies of this mystic Bird warbling in the loftiest heights of heaven. The Lord hath, in truth, inspired Me to proclaim: Verily, verily, I am God, He besides Whom there is none other God. He is the Almighty, the All-Wise.

O My servants! Seek ye earnestly this highest reward, as I have indeed created for the Remembrance of God gardens which remain inscrutable to anyone save Myself, and naught therein hath been made lawful unto anyone except those whose lives have been sacrificed in His Path. Hence beseech ye God, the Most Exalted, that He may grant you this meritorious reward, and He is in truth the Most High, the Most Great. Had it been Our wish, We would have brought all men into one fold round Our Remembrance, yet they will not cease to differ,[1] unless God accomplish what He willeth through the power of truth. In the estimation of the Remembrance this commandment hath, in very truth, been irrevocably ordained...

God hath indeed chosen Thee to warn the people, to guide the believers aright and to elucidate the secrets of the Book. *Chapter LXXXV.*

[1] cf. Qur'án 11:120

SHOULD it be Our wish, it is in Our power to compel, through the agency of but one letter of Our Revelation, the world and all that is therein to recognize, in less than the twinkling of an eye, the truth of Our Cause. . . .

Truly other apostles have been laughed to scorn before Thee,[1] and Thou art none other but the Servant of God, sustained by the power of Truth. Ere long We shall prolong the days of such as have rejected the Truth by reason of that which their hands have wrought,[2] and verily God will not deal unjustly with anyone, even to the extent of a speck on a date-stone. *Chapter LXXXVII.*

O YE peoples of the earth! By the righteousness of God, the True One, the testimony shown forth by His Remembrance is like unto a sun which the hand of the merciful Lord hath raised high in the midmost heart of the heaven, wherefrom it shineth in the plenitude of its meridian splendour . . .

With each and every Prophet Whom We have sent down in the past, We have established a separate Covenant concerning the Remembrance of God and His Day. Manifest, in the realm of glory and through the power of truth, are the Remembrance of God and His Day before the eyes of the angels that circle His mercy-seat. *Chapter XCI.*

[1] cf. Qur'án 6:10
[2] cf. ibid. 3:172

O HOUR of the Dawn! Ere the resplendent glory of the divine Luminary sheddeth its radiance from the Dayspring of this Gate, call thou to mind that the appointed Day of God will indeed be at hand in less than the twinkling of an eye. Thus hath the decree of God been issued in the Mother Book. *Chapter XCIV.*

O CONCOURSE of the faithful! Verily the object of each and every sign revealed by God in the Scriptures or in the world at large or in the hearts of men is but to make them fully realize that this Remembrance is indeed the True One from God. Verily God is cognizant of all things through the power of eternal Truth...

O ye that circle the throne of glory! Hearken unto My Call which is raised from the midst of the Burning Bush, 'Verily I am God and there is none other God but Me. Hence worship Me, and for the sake of Him Who is the Most Great Remembrance, offer ye prayers, purged from the insinuations of the people, for verily your Lord, the One true God, is none other than the Sovereign Truth. Indeed such as invoke others besides Him are deservedly numbered among the inmates of the fire, while He Who is the Remembrance of God verily abideth, firm and undeviating, on the Path of Truth amidst the Burning Bush.' ...

O peoples of the earth! Inflict not upon the Most Great Remembrance what the Umayyads cruelly inflicted upon Ḥusayn in the Holy Land. By the righteousness of God, the True One, He is indeed the Eternal Truth, and unto Him God, verily, is a witness. *Chapter XVII.*

GOD had, in truth, proposed Our Mission unto the heavens and the earth and the mountains, but they refused to bear it and were afraid thereof. However, Man, this 'Alí, Who is none other but the Great Remembrance of God, undertook to bear it. Hence God, the All-Encompassing, hath referred to Him in His Preserved Book as the 'Wronged One', and by reason of His being undistinguished before the eyes of men, He hath, according to the judgement of the Book, been entitled 'the Unknown' . . .[1]

Erelong We will, in very truth, torment such as waged war against Ḥusayn [Imám Ḥusayn], in the Land of the Euphrates, with the most afflictive torment, and the most dire and exemplary punishment. . . .

God knoweth well the heart of Ḥusayn, the heat of His burning thirst and His long-suffering for the sake of God, the Incomparable, the Ancient of Days; and unto Him God is verily a witness. *Chapter XII.*

HEARKEN unto the Voice of Thy Lord calling from Mount Sinai, 'Verily there is no God but Him, and I am the Most Exalted One Who hath been veiled in the Mother Book according to the dispensations of Providence.' *Chapter XIX.*

THIS Book which We have sent down is indeed abounding in blessings[2] and beareth witness to the Truth, so that

[1] cf. Qur'án 33:72
[2] cf. ibid. 6:93

the people may realize that the conclusive Proof of God in favour of His Remembrance is similar to the one wherewith Muḥammad, the Seal of the Prophets, was invested, and verily great is the Cause as ordained in the Mother Book. *Chapter LXVI.*

THIS Remembrance is indeed the glorious Remnant of the Light of God, and He will be best for you,[1] if ye in very truth remain faithful to God, the Most Exalted . . .

We have in truth sent Thee forth unto all men, by the leave of God, invested with Our signs and reinforced by Our unsurpassed sovereignty. He is indeed the appointed Bearer of the Trust of God . . .

O Qurratu'l-'Ayn! Persevere steadfastly as Thou art bidden and let not the faithless amongst men nor their utterances grieve Thee, since Thy Lord shall, by the righteousness of God, the Most Great, pass judgement upon them on the Day of Resurrection, and surely God witnesseth all things. *Chapter LXXXIV.*

THIS Religion is indeed, in the sight of God, the essence of the Faith of Muḥammad; haste ye then to attain the celestial Paradise and the all-highest Garden of His goodpleasure in the presence of the One True God, could ye but be patient and thankful before the evidences of the signs of God. *Chapter XLVIII.*

[1] cf. Qur'án 11:87

O MY servants! This is God's appointed Day which the merciful Lord hath promised you in His Book; wherefore, in very truth, glorify ye abundantly the name of God while treading the Path of the Most Great Remembrance . . .

Verily God hath granted leave to His Remembrance to say whatsoever He willeth in whatever manner He pleaseth. Indeed whatsoever He chooseth is none other than what is chosen by Us. The Lord, in truth, witnesseth all things. *Chapter LXXXVII.*

INDEED We conversed with Moses by the leave of God from the midst of the Burning Bush in the Sinai and revealed an infinitesimal glimmer of Thy Light upon the Mystic Mount and its dwellers, whereupon the Mount shook to its foundations and was crushed into dust . . .

O peoples of the earth! I swear by your Lord! Ye shall act as former generations have acted. Warn ye, then, yourselves of the terrible, the most grievous vengeance of God. For God is, verily, potent over all things. *Chapter LIII.*

O QURRATU'L-'AYN! I recognize in Thee none other except the 'Great Announcement'—the Announcement voiced by the Concourse on high. By this name, I bear witness, they that circle the Throne of Glory have ever known Thee.

O concourse of the believers! Do ye harbour any doubt

as to that whereunto the Remembrance of God doth summon you? By the righteousness of the One true God, He is none other than the sovereign Truth Who hath been made manifest through the power of Truth. Are ye in doubt concerning the Báb? Verily He is the One Who holdeth, by Our leave, the kingdoms of earth and heaven in His grasp, and the Lord is in truth fully aware of what ye are doing ...

Indeed I am but a man like unto you. However, God bestoweth upon Me whatever favours He willeth as He pleaseth,[1] and that which your Lord hath decreed in the Mother Book is unbounded. *Chapter LXXXVIII.*

God, of a truth, revealed unto Me in the sacred house of the Ka'bah, 'Verily, I am God, no God is there but Me. I have singled Thee out for Myself and have chosen Thee as the Remembrance. Indeed, whosoever beareth allegiance unto Thee by walking in the way of the Báb, for him the recompense of the next world hath surely been prescribed ...' It is ordained in the Book that upon the realization of the Cause of the Remembrance, the Most Great Event will have come to pass according to the dispensation of Providence, and God, truly, is potent over all things. *Chapter LXXIX.*

[1] cf. Qur'án 14:13

O QURRATU'L-'AYN! Say: Verily I am the One Who is hailed in the Mother Book as the 'Great Announcement'. Say: The people have grievously differed over Me, whereas in truth there is no difference between Me and the Báb; and God, the Eternal Truth, is sufficient witness. *Chapter LXXVII.*

I AM the Mystic Fane which the Hand of Omnipotence hath reared. I am the Lamp which the Finger of God hath lit within its niche and caused to shine with deathless splendour. I am the Flame of that supernal Light that glowed upon Sinai in the gladsome Spot, and lay concealed in the midst of the Burning Bush. *Chapter XCIV.*

As a token of pure justice, We have indeed sent tidings unto every Prophet concerning the Cause of Our Remembrance, and verily God is supreme over all the peoples of the world. *Chapter LXXXIII.*

3

EXCERPTS FROM THE PERSIAN BAYÁN

IT is better to guide one soul than to possess all that is on earth, for as long as that guided soul is under the shadow of the Tree of Divine Unity, he and the one who hath guided him will both be recipients of God's tender mercy, whereas possession of earthly things will cease at the time of death. The path to guidance is one of love and compassion, not of force and coercion. This hath been God's method in the past, and shall continue to be in the future! He causeth him whom He pleaseth to enter the shadow of His Mercy. Verily, He is the Supreme Protector, the All-Generous.

There is no paradise more wondrous for any soul than to be exposed to God's Manifestation in His Day, to hear His verses and believe in them, to attain His presence, which is naught but the presence of God, to sail upon the sea of the heavenly kingdom of His good-pleasure, and to partake of the choice fruits of the paradise of His divine Oneness. *II, 16.*[1]

WORSHIP thou God in such wise that if thy worship lead thee to the fire, no alteration in thine adoration would be produced, and so likewise if thy recompense should be paradise. Thus and thus alone should be the worship which befitteth the one True God. Shouldst thou worship Him because of fear, this would be unseemly in the sanctified Court of His presence, and could not be regarded as an act by thee dedicated to the Oneness of His Being. Or if thy

---

[1] The Bayán is divided into váhids and chapters, to which these numbers refer.

gaze should be on paradise, and thou shouldst worship Him while cherishing such a hope, thou wouldst make God's creation a partner with Him, notwithstanding the fact that paradise is desired by men.

Fire and paradise both bow down and prostrate themselves before God. That which is worthy of His Essence is to worship Him for His sake, without fear of fire, or hope of paradise.

Although when true worship is offered, the worshipper is delivered from the fire, and entereth the paradise of God's good-pleasure, yet such should not be the motive of his act. However, God's favour and grace ever flow in accordance with the exigencies of His inscrutable wisdom.

The most acceptable prayer is the one offered with the utmost spirituality and radiance; its prolongation hath not been and is not beloved by God. The more detached and the purer the prayer, the more acceptable is it in the presence of God. *VII, 19*.

THE Day of Resurrection is a day on which the sun riseth and setteth like unto any other day. How oft hath the Day of Resurrection dawned, and the people of the land where it occurred did not learn of the event. Had they heard, they would not have believed, and thus they were not told!

When the Apostle of God [Muḥammad] appeared, He did not announce unto the unbelievers that the Resurrection had come, for they could not bear the news. That Day is indeed an infinitely mighty Day, for in it the Divine Tree proclaimeth from eternity unto eternity, 'Verily, I am God. No God is there but Me'. Yet those who are veiled believe that He is one like unto them, and they refuse even to call Him a believer, although such a title in the realm of His heavenly Kingdom is conferred everlastingly upon the most insignificant follower of His previous Dispensation. Thus, had the people in the days of the Apostle of God regarded Him at least as a believer of their time how would they have debarred Him, for seven years while He was in the mountain, from access to His Holy House [Ka'bah]? Likewise in this Dispensation of the Point of the Bayán, if the people had not refused to concede the name believer unto Him, how could they have incarcerated Him on this mountain, without realizing that the quintessence of belief oweth its existence to a word from Him? Their hearts are deprived of the power of true insight, and thus they cannot see, while those endowed with the eyes of the spirit circle like moths round the Light of Truth until they are consumed. It is for this reason that the Day of Resurrection is said to be the greatest of all days, yet it is like unto any other day. *VIII, 9.*

THERE is no paradise, in the estimation of the believers in the Divine Unity, more exalted than to obey God's commandments, and there is no fire in the eyes of those who have known God and His signs, fiercer than to transgress His laws and to oppress another soul, even to the extent of a mustard seed. On the Day of Resurrection God will, in truth, judge all men, and we all verily plead for His grace. *V, 19.*

God loveth those who are pure. Naught in the Bayán and in the sight of God is more loved than purity and immaculate cleanliness. . . .

God desireth not to see, in the Dispensation of the Bayán, any soul deprived of joy and radiance. He indeed desireth that under all conditions, all may be adorned with such purity, both inwardly and outwardly, that no repugnance may be caused even to themselves, how much less unto others. *V, 14.*

Likewise consider the manifestation of the Point of the Bayán. There are people who every night until morning busy themselves with the worship of God, and even at present when the Day-Star of Truth is nearing its zenith in the heaven of its Revelation, they have not yet left their prayer-rugs. If any one of them ever heard the wondrous verses of God recited unto him, he would exclaim: 'Why dost thou keep me back from offering my prayers?' O thou who art wrapt in veils! If thou makest mention of God, wherefore sufferest thou thyself to be shut out from Him Who hath kindled the light of worship in thy heart? If He had not previously revealed the injunction: 'Verily, make ye mention of God'[1], what would have prompted thee to offer devotion unto God, and whereunto wouldst thou turn in prayer?

Know thou of a certainty that whenever thou makest mention of Him Whom God shall make manifest, only then art thou making mention of God. In like manner shouldst thou hearken unto the verses of the Bayán and

[1] Qur'án 8:47; 33:41; 62:10

acknowledge its truth, only then would the revealed verses of God profit thee. Otherwise what benefit canst thou derive therefrom? For wert thou to prostrate thyself in adoration from the beginning of life till the end and to spend thy days for the sake of God's remembrance, but disbelieve in the Exponent of His Revelation for the age, dost thou imagine that thy deeds would confer any benefit upon thee? On the other hand, if thou believest in Him and dost recognize Him with true understanding, and He saith: 'I have accepted thine entire life spent in My adoration', then assuredly hast thou been worshipping Him most ardently. Thy purpose in performing thy deeds is that God may graciously accept them; and divine acceptance can in no wise be achieved except through the acceptance of Him Who is the Exponent of His Revelation. For instance, if the Apostle of God—may divine blessings rest upon Him—accepted a certain deed, in truth God accepted it; otherwise it hath remained within the selfish desires of the person who wrought it, and did not reach the presence of God. Likewise, any act which is accepted by the Point of the Bayán is accepted by God, inasmuch as the contingent world hath no other access unto the presence of the Ancient of Days. Whatever is sent down cometh through the Exponent of His Revelation, and whatever ascendeth, ascendeth unto the Exponent of His Revelation. *VIII, 19.*

There is no doubt that the Almighty hath sent down these verses unto Him [the Báb], even as He sent down unto the Apostle of God. Indeed no less than a hundred thousand verses similar to these have already been disseminated among the people, not to mention His Epistles, His Prayers or His learned and philosophical treatises. He revealeth no less than a thousand verses within the space of five hours. He reciteth verses at a speed consonant with the capacity of His amanuensis to set them down. Thus, it may well be considered that if from the inception of this Revelation until now He had been left unhindered, how vast then would have been the volume of writings disseminated from His pen.

If ye contend that these verses cannot, of themselves, be regarded as a proof, scan the pages of the Qur'án. If God hath established therein any evidence other than the revealed verses to demonstrate the validity of the prophethood of His Apostle—may the blessings of God rest upon Him—ye may then have your scruples about Him . . .

Concerning the sufficiency of the Book as a proof, God hath revealed: 'Is it not enough for them that We have sent down unto Thee the Book to be recited to them? In this verily is a mercy and a warning to those who believe.'[1] When God hath testified that the Book is a sufficient testimony, as is affirmed in the text, how can one dispute this truth by saying that the Book in itself is not a conclusive proof? . . . *II, 1*.

SINCE that Day is a great Day it would be sorely trying for thee to identify thyself with the believers. For the believers of that Day are the inmates of Paradise, while the unbelievers are the inmates of the fire. And know thou of a certainty that by Paradise is meant recognition of and sub-

[1] Qur'án 29:50

mission unto Him Whom God shall make manifest, and by the fire the company of such souls as would fail to submit unto Him or to be resigned to His good-pleasure. On that Day thou wouldst regard thyself as the inmate of Paradise and as a true believer in Him, whereas in reality thou wouldst suffer thyself to be wrapt in veils and thy habitation would be the nethermost fire, though thou thyself wouldst not be cognizant thereof.

Compare His manifestation with that of the Point of the Qur'án. How vast the number of the Letters of the Gospel who eagerly expected Him, yet from the time of His declaration up to five years no one became an inmate of Paradise, except the Commander of the Faithful [Imám 'Alí], and those who secretly believed in Him. All the rest were accounted as inmates of the fire, though they considered themselves as dwellers in Paradise.

Likewise behold this Revelation. The essences of the people have, through divinely-conceived designs, been set in motion and until the present day three hundred and thirteen disciples have been chosen. In the land of Ṣád [Iṣfáhán], which to outward seeming is a great city, in every corner of whose seminaries are vast numbers of people regarded as divines and doctors, yet when the time came for inmost essences to be drawn forth, only its sifter of wheat donned the robe of discipleship. This is the mystery of what was uttered by the kindred of the Prophet Muḥammad—upon them be the peace of God— concerning this Revelation, saying that the abased shall be exalted and the exalted shall be abased.

Likewise is the Revelation of Him Whom God shall make manifest. Among those to whom it will never occur that they might merit the displeasure of God, and whose pious deeds will be exemplary unto everyone, there will be many who will become the personification of the nether-most fire itself, when they fail to embrace His Cause; while among the lowly servants whom no one would imagine to be of any merit, how great the number who will be honoured with true faith and on whom the Fountainhead of generosity will bestow the robe of authority. For whatever is created in the Faith of God is created through the potency of His Word. *VIII, 14.*

I N the manifestation of the Apostle of God all were eagerly awaiting Him, yet thou hast heard how He was treated at the time of His appearance, in spite of the fact that if ever they beheld Him in their dreams they would take pride in them.

Likewise in the manifestation of the Point of the Bayán, the people stood up at the mention of His Name and fervently implored His advent night and day, and if they dreamt of Him they gloried in their dreams; yet now that He hath revealed Himself, invested with the mightiest testimony, whereby their own religion is vindicated, and despite the incalculable number of people who yearningly anticipate His coming, they are resting comfortably in their homes, after having hearkened to His verses; while He at this moment is confined in the mountain of Mákú, lonely and forsaken.

Take good heed of yourselves, O people of the Bayán, lest ye perform such deeds as to weep sore for His sake night and day, to stand up at the mention of His Name, yet on this Day of fruition—a Day whereon ye should not only arise at His Name, but seek a path unto Him Who personifies that Name—ye shut yourselves out from Him as by a veil. *VI, 15.*

At the time of the manifestation of Him Whom God shall make manifest everyone should be well trained in the teachings of the Bayán, so that none of the followers may outwardly cling to the Bayán and thus forfeit their allegiance unto Him. If anyone does so, the verdict of 'disbeliever in God' shall be passed upon him.

I swear by the holy Essence of God, were all in the Bayán to unite in helping Him Whom God shall make manifest in the days of His Revelation, not a single soul, nay, not a created thing would remain on earth that would not gain admittance into Paradise. Take good heed of yourselves, for the sum total of the religion of God is but to help Him, rather than to observe, in the time of His appearance, such deeds as are prescribed in the Bayán. Should anyone, however, ere He manifesteth Himself, transgress the ordinances, were it to the extent of a grain of barley, he would have transgressed His command.

Seek ye refuge in God from whatsoever might lead you astray from the Source of His Revelation and hold fast unto His Cord, for whoso holdeth fast unto His allegiance, he hath attained and will attain salvation in all the worlds.

'Such is the bounty of God; to whom He will, He giveth it, and God is the Lord of grace abounding.'[1] *V, 5.*

[1] Qur'án 57:21

YE perform your works for God from the beginning of your lives till the end thereof, yet not a single act is for the sake of Him Who is the Manifestation of God, to Whom every good deed reverteth. Had ye acted in such manner, ye would not have suffered so grievously on the Day of Resurrection.

Behold how great is the Cause, and yet how the people are wrapt in veils. I swear by the sanctified Essence of God that every true praise and deed offered unto God is naught but praise and deed offered unto Him Whom God shall make manifest.

Deceive not your own selves that you are being virtuous for the sake of God when you are not. For should ye truly do your works for God, ye would be performing them for Him Whom God shall make manifest and would be magnifying His Name. The dwellers of this mountain who are bereft of true understanding unceasingly utter the words, 'No God is there but God'; but what benefit doth it yield them? Ponder awhile that ye may not be shut out as by a veil from Him Who is the Dayspring of Revelation. *VIII, 19.*

GOD hath, at all times and under all conditions, been wholly independent of His creatures. He hath cherished and will ever cherish the desire that all men may attain His gardens of Paradise with utmost love, that no one should sadden another, not even for a moment, and that all should dwell within His cradle of protection and security until the Day of Resurrection which marketh the dayspring of the Revelation of Him Whom God will make manifest.

The Lord of the universe hath never raised up a prophet nor hath He sent down a Book unless He hath established His covenant with all men, calling for their acceptance of the next Revelation and of the next Book; inasmuch as the outpourings of His bounty are ceaseless and without limit. *VI, 16.*

How veiled are ye, O My creatures,[1] . . . who, without any right, have consigned Him unto a mountain [Mákú], not one of whose inhabitants is worthy of mention . . . With Him, which is with Me, there is no one except him who is one of the Letters of the Living of My Book. In His presence, which is My Presence, there is not at night even a lighted lamp! And yet, in places [of worship] which in varying degrees reach out unto Him, unnumbered lamps are shining! All that is on earth hath been created for Him, and all partake with delight of His benefits, and yet they are so veiled from Him as to refuse Him even a lamp!

In this Day therefore I bear witness unto My creatures, for the witness of no one other than Myself hath been or shall ever be worthy of mention in My presence. I affirm that no Paradise is more sublime for My creatures than to stand before My face and to believe in My holy Words, while no fire hath been or will be fiercer for them than to be veiled from the Manifestation of My exalted Self and to disbelieve in My Words.

Ye may contend: 'How doth He speak on Our behalf?'

[1] In *The Promised Day is Come* on page 7 Shoghi Effendi affirms that this passage was revealed by the Báb speaking with the voice of God.

Have ye not perused the unseemly words ye uttered in the past, as reflected in the text of My Book, and still ye feel not ashamed? Ye have now seen the truth of My Book conclusively established and today every one of you doth profess belief in Me through that Book. The day is not far distant when ye shall readily realize that your glory lieth in your belief in these holy verses. Today, however, when only belief in this Faith truly profiteth you, ye have debarred yourselves therefrom by reason of the things which are disadvantageous unto you and will inflict harm upon you, whereas He Who is the Manifestation of My Self hath been and shall ever remain immune from any harm whatever, and any loss that hath appeared or will appear shall eventually revert unto yourselves. *II, 1.*

How vast the number of people who are well versed in every science, yet it is their adherence to the holy Word of God which will determine their faith, inasmuch as the fruit of every science is none other than the knowledge of divine precepts and submission unto His good-pleasure. *II, 1.*

No created thing shall ever attain its paradise unless it appeareth in its highest prescribed degree of perfection. For instance, this crystal representeth the paradise of the stone whereof its substance is composed. Likewise there are various stages in the paradise for the crystal itself . . . So long as it was stone it was worthless, but if it attaineth

the excellence of ruby—a potentiality which is latent in it—
how much a carat will it be worth? Consider likewise every
created thing.

Man's highest station, however, is attained through
faith in God in every Dispensation and by acceptance of
what hath been revealed by Him, and not through learning; inasmuch as in every nation there are learned men who
are versed in divers sciences. Nor is it attainable through
wealth; for it is similarly evident that among the various
classes in every nation there are those possessed of riches.
Likewise are other transitory things.

True knowledge, therefore, is the knowledge of God,
and this is none other than the recognition of His Manifestation in each Dispensation. Nor is there any wealth
save in poverty in all save God and sanctity from aught else
but Him—a state that can be realized only when demonstrated towards Him Who is the Dayspring of His Revelation. This doth not mean, however, that one ought not
to yield praise unto former Revelations. On no account is
this acceptable, inasmuch as it behooveth man, upon
reaching the age of nineteen, to render thanksgiving for the
day of his conception as an embryo. For had the embryo
not existed, how could he have reached his present state?
Likewise had the religion taught by Adam not existed,
this Faith would not have attained its present stage. Thus
consider thou the development of God's Faith until the
end that hath no end. *V, 4.*

T WELVE hundred and seventy years have elapsed since
the declaration of Muḥammad, and each year unnumbered

people have circumambulated the House of God [Mecca].
In the concluding year of this period He Who is Himself
the Founder of the House went on pilgrimage. Great God!
There was a vast concourse of pilgrims from every sect.
Yet not one recognized Him, though He recognized every
one of them—souls tightly held in the grasp of His former
commandment. The only person who recognized Him and
performed pilgrimage with Him is the one round whom
revolve eight Váḥids,[1] in whom God hath gloried before
the Concourse on high by virtue of his absolute detachment and for his being wholly devoted to the Will of God.
This doth not mean that he was made the object of a special
favour, nay, this is a favour which God hath vouchsafed
unto all men, yet they have suffered themselves to be veiled
from it. The Commentary on the Súrih of Joseph had, in
the first year of this Revelation, been widely distributed.
Nevertheless, when the people realized that fellow supporters were not forthcoming they hesitated to accept it;
while it never occurred to them that the very Qur'án
whereunto unnumbered souls bear fealty today, was
revealed in the midmost heart of the Arab world, yet to
outward seeming for no less than seven years no one acknowledged its truth except the Commander of the Faithful
[Imám 'Alí]—may the peace of God rest upon him—who,
in response to the conclusive proofs advanced by God's
supreme Testimony, recognized the Truth and did not fix
his eyes on others. Thus on the Day of Resurrection God
will ask everyone of his understanding and not of his
following in the footsteps of others. How often a person,
having inclined his ears to the holy verses, would bow

---

[1] This is a reference to Quddús, 'whom the Persian Bayán
extolled as that fellow-pilgrim round whom mirrors to the
number of eight Váḥids revolve'. (*God Passes By*, p. 49).

down in humility and would embrace the Truth, while his leader would not do so. Thus every individual must bear his own responsibility, rather than someone else bearing it for him. At the time of the appearance of Him Whom God will make manifest the most distinguished among the learned and the lowliest of men shall both be judged alike. How often the most insignificant of men have acknowledged the truth, while the most learned have remained wrapt in veils. Thus in every Dispensation a number of souls enter the fire by reason of their following in the footsteps of others. *IV, 18.*

Better is it for a person to write down but one of His verses than to transcribe the whole of the Bayán and all the books which have been written in the Dispensation of the Bayán. For everything shall be set aside except His Writings, which will endure until the following Revelation. And should anyone inscribe with true faith but one letter of that Revelation, his recompense would be greater than for inscribing all the heavenly Writings of the past and all that has been written during previous Dispensations. Likewise continue thou to ascend through one Revelation after another, knowing that thy progress in the Knowledge of God shall never come to an end, even as it can have no beginning. *VII, 13.*

O PEOPLE of the Bayán! Be on your guard; for on the Day of Resurrection no one shall find a place to flee to. He will shine forth suddenly, and will pronounce judgement as He pleaseth. If it be His wish He will cause the abased to be exalted, and the exalted to be abased, even as He did in the Bayán, couldst thou but understand. And no one but Him is equal unto this. Whatever He ordaineth will be fulfilled, and nothing will remain unfulfilled. *VII, 9.*

SINCE all men have issued forth from the shadow of the signs of His Divinity and Lordship, they always tend to take a path, lofty and high. And because they are bereft of a discerning eye to recognize their Beloved, they fall short of their duty to manifest meekness and humility towards Him. Nevertheless, from the beginning of their lives till the end thereof, in conformity with the laws established in the previous religion, they worship God, piously adore Him, bow themselves before His divine Reality and show submissiveness toward His exalted Essence. At the hour of His manifestation, however, they all turn their gaze toward their own selves and are thus shut out from Him, inasmuch as they fancifully regard Him as one like unto themselves. Far from the glory of God is such a comparison. Indeed that august Being resembleth the physical sun, His verses are like its rays, and all believers, should they truly believe in Him, are as mirrors wherein the sun is reflected. Their light is thus a mere reflection. *VII, 15.*

O PEOPLE of the Bayán! If ye believe in Him Whom God shall make manifest, to your own behoof do ye believe. He hath been and ever will remain independent of all men. For instance, were ye to place unnumbered mirrors before the sun, they would all reflect the sun and produce impressions thereof, whereas the sun is in itself wholly independent of the existence of the mirrors and of the suns which they reproduce. Such are the bounds of the contingent beings in their relation to the manifestation of the Eternal Being . . .

In this day no less than seventy thousand people make pilgrimage every year to the holy House of God in compliance with the bidding of the Apostle of God; while He Himself Who ordained this ordinance took refuge for seven years in the mountains of Mecca. And this notwithstanding that the One Who enjoined this commandment is far greater than the commandment itself. Hence all this people who at this time go on pilgrimage do not do so with true understanding, otherwise in this Day of His Return which is mightier than His former Dispensation, they would have followed His commandment. But now behold what hath happened. People who profess belief in His former religion, who in the daytime and in the night season bow down in worship in His Name, have assigned Him to a dwelling place in a mountain, while each one of them would regard attaining recognition of Him as an honour. *VII, 15.*

THE reason why privacy hath been enjoined in moments of devotion is this, that thou mayest give thy best attention to the remembrance of God, that thy heart may at all times be animated with His Spirit, and not be shut out as by a veil from thy Best Beloved. Let not thy tongue pay lip service in praise of God while thy heart be not attuned to the exalted Summit of Glory, and the Focal Point of communion. Thus if haply thou dost live in the Day of Resurrection, the mirror of thy heart will be set towards Him Who is the Day-Star of Truth; and no sooner will His light shine forth than the splendour thereof shall forthwith be reflected in thy heart. For He is the Source of all goodness, and unto Him revert all things. But if He appeareth while thou hast turned unto thyself in meditation, this shall not profit thee, unless thou shalt mention His Name by words He hath revealed. For in the forthcoming Revelation it is He Who is the Remembrance of God, whereas the devotions which thou art offering at present have been prescribed by the Point of the Bayán, while He Who will shine resplendent in the Day of Resurrection is the Revelation of the inner reality enshrined in the Point of the Bayán —a Revelation more potent, immeasurably more potent, than the one which hath preceded it. *IX, 4.*

It is seemly that the servant should, after each prayer, supplicate God to bestow mercy and forgiveness upon his parents. Thereupon God's call will be raised: 'Thousand upon thousand of what thou hast asked for thy parents shall be thy recompense!' Blessed is he who remembereth his parents when communing with God. There is, verily, no God but Him, the Mighty, the Well-Beloved. *VIII, 16.*

As this physical frame is the throne of the inner temple, whatever occurs to the former is felt by the latter. In reality that which takes delight in joy or is saddened by pain is the inner temple of the body, not the body itself. Since this physical body is the throne whereon the inner temple is established, God hath ordained that the body be preserved to the extent possible, so that nothing that causeth repugnance may be experienced. The inner temple beholdeth its physical frame, which is its throne. Thus, if the latter is accorded respect, it is as if the former is the recipient. The converse is likewise true.

Therefore, it hath been ordained that the dead body should be treated with the utmost honour and respect. *V*, *12*.

At the time of the appearance of Him Whom God shall make manifest, wert thou to perform thy deeds for the sake of the Point of the Bayán, they would be regarded as performed for one other than God, inasmuch as on that Day the Point of the Bayán is none other than Him Whom God shall make manifest . . .

It is for this reason that at the beginning of every Dispensation a vast multitude, who fondly imagine that their deeds are for God, become drowned and ungodly, and perceive this not, except such as He guideth at His behest.

It is better for a man to guide a soul than to possess all that lies between East and West. Likewise better is guidance for him who is guided than all the things that exist on earth, for by reason of this guidance he will, after his death, gain admittance into Paradise, whereas by reason of the things of the world below, he will, after his death, receive his deserts. Hence God desireth that all men should be guided aright through the potency of the Words of Him Whom God shall make manifest. However, such as are conceited will not suffer themselves to be guided. They will be debarred from the Truth, some by reason of their learning, others on account of their glory and power, and still others due to reasons of their own, none of which shall be of any avail at the hour of death.

Take ye good heed that ye may all, under the leadership of Him Who is the Source of Divine Guidance, be enabled to direct your steps aright upon the Bridge, which is sharper than the sword and finer than a hair, so that perchance the things which from the beginning of thy life till the end thou hast performed for the love of God, may not, all at once and unrealized by thyself, be turned to acts not acceptable in the sight of God. Verily God guideth whom He will into the path of absolute certitude. *VII, 2.*

E VERYONE is eagerly awaiting His appearance, yet since their inner eyes are not directed towards Him sorrow must needs befall Him. In the case of the Apostle of God—may the blessings of God rest upon Him—before the revelation of the Qur'án everyone bore witness to His piety and noble virtues. Behold Him then after the revelation of the Qur'án. What outrageous insults were levelled against Him, as indeed the pen is ashamed to recount. Likewise behold the Point of the Bayán. His behaviour prior to the declaration of His mission is clearly evident unto those who knew Him. Now, following His manifestation, although He hath, up to the present, revealed no less than five hundred thousand verses on different subjects, behold what calumnies are uttered, so unseemly that the pen is stricken with shame at the mention of them. But if all men were to observe the ordinances of God no sadness would befall that heavenly Tree. *VI, 11.*

T HE acts of Him Whom God shall make manifest are like unto the sun, while the works of men, provided they conform to the good-pleasure of God, resemble the stars or the moon . . . Thus, should the followers of the Bayán observe the precepts of Him Whom God shall make manifest at the time of His appearance, and regard themselves and their own works as stars exposed to the light of the sun, then they will have gathered the fruits of their existence; otherwise the title of 'starship' will not apply to them. Rather it will apply to such as truly believe in Him, to those who pale into insignificance in the day-time and gleam forth with light in the night season.

Such indeed is the fruit of this precept, should anyone observe it on the Day of Resurrection. This is the essence of all learning and of all righteous deeds, should anyone but attain unto it. Had the peoples of the world fixed their gaze upon this principle, no Exponent of divine Revelation would ever have, at the inception of any Dispensation, regarded them as things of naught. However, the fact is that during the night season everyone perceiveth the light which he himself, according to his own capacity, giveth out, oblivious that at the break of day this light shall fade away and be reduced to utter nothingness before the dazzling splendour of the sun.

The light of the people of the world is their knowledge and utterance; while the splendours shed from the glorious acts of Him Whom God shall make manifest are His Words, through whose potency He rolleth up the whole world of existence, sets it under His Own authority by relating it unto Himself, then as the Mouthpiece of God, the Source of His divine light—exalted and glorified be He —proclaimeth: 'Verily, verily, I am God, no God is there but Me; in truth all others except Me are My creatures. Say, O My creatures! Me alone, therefore, should ye fear'. *VIII, 1.*

Know thou that in the Bayán purification is regarded as the most acceptable means for attaining nearness unto God and as the most meritorious of all deeds. Thus purge thou thine ear that thou mayest hear no mention besides God, and purge thine eye that it behold naught except God, and thy conscience that it perceive naught other than God, and thy tongue that it proclaim nothing but God, and thy hand to write naught but the words of God, and thy knowledge that it comprehend naught except God, and thy heart that it entertain no wish save God, and in like manner purge all thine acts and thy pursuits that thou mayest be nurtured in the paradise of pure love, and perchance mayest attain the presence of Him Whom God shall make manifest, adorned with a purity which He highly cherisheth, and be sanctified from whosoever hath turned away from Him and doth not support Him. Thus shalt thou manifest a purity that shall profit thee.

Know thou that every ear which hearkeneth unto His

Words with true faith shall be immune from the fire. Thus the believer, through his recognition of Him will appreciate the transcendent character of His heavenly Words, will whole-heartedly choose Him over others, and will refuse to incline his affections towards those who disbelieve in Him. Whatever one gaineth in the life to come is but the fruit of this faith. Indeed any man whose eye gazeth upon His Words with true faith well deserveth Paradise; and one whose conscience beareth witness unto His Words with true faith shall abide in Paradise and attain the presence of God; and one whose tongue giveth utterance to His Words with true faith shall have his abode in Paradise, wherein he will be seized with ecstasy in praise and glorification of God, the Ever-Abiding, Whose revelations of glory never end and the reviving breaths of Whose holiness never fail. Every hand which setteth down His Words with true faith shall be filled by God, both in this world and in the next, with things that are highly prized; and every breast which committeth His Words to memory, God shall cause, if it were that of a believer, to be filled with His love; and every heart which cherisheth the love of His Words and manifesteth in itself the signs of true faith when His Name is mentioned, and exemplifieth the words, 'their hearts are thrilled with awe at the mention of God',[1] that heart will become the object of the glances of divine favour and on the Day of Resurrection will be highly praised by God. *IX, 10.*

[1] Qur'án 8:2

I F at the time of the appearance of Him Whom God will make manifest all the dwellers of the earth were to bear witness unto a thing whereunto He beareth witness differently, His testimony would be like unto the sun, while theirs would be even as a false image produced in a mirror which is not facing the sun. For had it been otherwise their testimony would have proved a faithful reflection of His testimony.

I swear by the most sacred Essence of God that but one line of the Words uttered by Him is more sublime than the words uttered by all that dwell on earth. Nay, I beg forgiveness for making this comparison. How could the reflections of the sun in the mirror compare with the wondrous rays of the sun in the visible heaven? The station of one is that of nothingness, while the station of the other, by the righteousness of God—hallowed and magnified be His Name—is that of the Reality of things. . . .

If in the Day of His manifestation a king were to make mention of his own sovereignty, this would be like unto a mirror challenging the sun, saying: 'The light is in me'. It would be likewise, if a man of learning in His Day were to claim to be an exponent of knowledge, or if he who is possessed of riches were to display his affluence, or if a man wielding power were to assert his own authority, or if one invested with grandeur were to show forth his glory. Nay, such men would become the object of the derision of their peers, and how would they be judged by Him Who is the Sun of Truth! *III, 12.*

It is not permissible to ask questions from Him Whom God will make manifest, except that which well beseemeth Him. For His station is that of the Essence of divine Revelation . . . Whatever evidence of bounty is witnessed in the world, is but an image of His bounty; and every thing owes its existence to His Being . . . The Bayán is, from beginning to end, the repository of all of His attributes, and the treasury of both His fire and His light. Should anyone desire to ask questions, he is allowed to do so only in writing, that he may derive ample understanding from His written reply and that it may serve as a sign from his Beloved. However, let no one ask aught that may prove unworthy of His lofty station. For instance, were a person to inquire the price of straw from a merchant of rubies, how ignorant would he be and how unacceptable. Similarly unacceptable would be the questions of the highest-ranking people of the world in His presence, except such words as He Himself would utter about Himself in the Day of His manifestation.

Methinks I visualize those who would, prompted by their own deluded conceptions, write to Him and ask Him questions about that which hath been revealed in the Bayán, and He would answer them with words not of His Own, but divinely inspired, saying: 'Verily, verily, I am God; no God is there but Me. I have called into being all the created things, I have raised up divine Messengers in the past and have sent down Books unto Them. Take heed not to worship anyone but God, He Who is My Lord and your Lord. This indeed is the undoubted truth. However, alike shall it be to Me; if ye believe in Me, ye will provide good for your own souls, and if ye believe not in Me, nor in that which God hath revealed unto Me, ye will suffer yourselves to be shut out as by a veil. For verily I have been independent of you heretofore, and shall remain independent hereafter. Therefore it behooveth you, O creatures of God, to help your own selves and to believe in the Verses revealed by Me...' *III, 13.*

THE Bayán shall constitute God's unerring balance till the Day of Resurrection which is the Day of Him Whom God will make manifest. Whoso acteth in conformity with that which is revealed therein will abide in Paradise, under the shadow of His affirmation and reckoned among the most sublime Letters in the presence of God; while whoso deviateth, were it even so much as the tip of a grain of barley, will be consigned to the fire and will be assembled neath the shadow of negation. This truth hath likewise been laid bare in the Qur'án where in numerous instances God hath set down that whoever should pass judgement contrary to the bounds fixed by Him, would be deemed an infidel...

In these days how few are those who abide by the standard laid down in the Qur'án. Nay, nowhere are they to be found, except such as God hath willed. Should there be, however, such a person, his righteous deeds would prove of no avail unto him, if he hath failed to follow the standard revealed in the Bayán; even as the pious deeds of the Christian monks profited them not, inasmuch as at the time of the manifestation of the Apostle of God—may the blessings of God rest upon Him—they contented themselves with the standard set forth in the Gospel.

Had the divine standard laid down in the Qur'án been truly observed, adverse judgements would not have been pronounced against Him Who is the Tree of divine Truth.

As it hath been revealed: 'Almost might the heavens be rent and the earth be cleft asunder and the mountains fall down in fragments.'[1] And yet how much harder than these mountains their hearts must be to have remained unmoved! Indeed no paradise is more glorious in the sight of God than attainment unto His good-pleasure. *II, 6.*

THE One true God may be compared unto the sun and the believer unto a mirror. No sooner is the mirror placed before the sun than it reflects its light. The unbeliever may be likened unto a stone. No matter how long it is exposed to the sunshine, it cannot reflect the sun. Thus the former layeth down his life as a sacrifice, while the latter doeth against God what he committeth. Indeed, if God willeth, He is potent to turn the stone into a mirror, but the person himself remaineth reconciled to his state. Had he wished to become a crystal, God would have made him to assume crystal form. For on that Day whatever cause prompteth the believer to believe in Him, the same will also be available to the unbeliever. But when the latter suffereth himself to be wrapt in veils, the same cause shutteth him out as by a veil. Thus, as is clearly evident today, those who have set their faces toward God, the True One, have believed in Him because of the Bayán, while such as are veiled have been deprived because of it. *VI, 4.*

[1] Qur'án 19:92

I SWEAR by the most holy Essence of God—exalted and glorified be He—that in the Day of the appearance of Him Whom God shall make manifest a thousand perusals of the Bayán cannot equal the perusal of a single verse to be revealed by Him Whom God shall make manifest.

Ponder a while and observe that everything in Islám hath its ultimate and eventual beginning in the Book of God. Consider likewise the Day of the Revelation of Him Whom God shall make manifest, He in Whose grasp lieth the source of proofs, and let not erroneous considerations shut thee out from Him, for He is immeasurably exalted above them, inasmuch as every proof proceedeth from the Book of God which is itself the supreme testimony, as all men are powerless to produce its like. Should myriads of men of learning, versed in logic, in the science of grammar, in law, in jurisprudence and the like, turn away from the Book of God, they would still be pronounced unbelievers. Thus the fruit is within the supreme testimony itself, not in the things derived therefrom. And know thou of a certainty that every letter revealed in the Bayán is solely intended to evoke submission unto Him Whom God shall make manifest, for it is He Who hath revealed the Bayán prior to His Own manifestation. *V, 8.*

IN this Revelation the Lord of the universe hath deigned to bestow His mighty utterances and resplendent signs upon the Point of the Bayán, and hath ordained them as His matchless testimony for all created things. Were all the people that dwell on earth to assemble together, they would be unable to produce a single verse like unto the ones which

God hath caused to stream forth from the tongue of the Point of the Bayán. Indeed, if any living creature were to pause to meditate he would undoubtedly realize that these verses are not the work of man, but are solely to be ascribed unto God, the One, the Peerless, Who causeth them to flow forth from the tongue of whomsoever He willeth, and hath not revealed nor will He reveal them save through the Focal Point of God's Primal Will. He it is, through Whose dispensations divine Messengers are raised up and heavenly Books are sent down. Had human beings been able to accomplish this deed surely someone would have brought forth at least one verse during the period of twelve hundred and seventy years which hath elapsed since the revelation of the Qur'án until that of the Bayán. However, all men have proved themselves impotent and have utterly failed to do so, although they endeavoured, with their vehement might, to quench the flame of the Word of God. *II*, *1*.

THOU beholdest how vast is the number of people who go to Mecca each year on pilgrimage and engage in circumambulation, while He, through the potency of Whose Word the Ka'bah [the sanctuary in Mecca] hath become the object of adoration, is forsaken in this mountain. He is none other but the Apostle of God Himself, inasmuch as the Revelation of God may be likened to the sun. No matter how innumerable its risings, there is but one sun, and upon it depends the life of all things. It is clear and evident that the object of all preceding Dispensations hath been to pave the way for the advent of Muḥammad, the Apostle of God.

These, including the Muḥammadan Dispensation, have had, in their turn, as their objective the Revelation proclaimed by the Qá'im. The purpose underlying this Revelation, as well as those that preceded it, has, in like manner, been to announce the advent of the Faith of Him Whom God will make manifest. And this Faith—the Faith of Him Whom God will make manifest—in its turn, together with all the Revelations gone before it, have as their object the Manifestation destined to succeed it. And the latter, no less than all the Revelations preceding it, prepare the way for the Revelation which is yet to follow. The process of the rise and setting of the Sun of Truth will thus indefinitely continue—a process that hath had no beginning and will have no end.

Well is it with him who in every Dispensation recognizeth the Purpose of God for that Dispensation, and is not deprived therefrom by turning his gaze towards the things of the past. *IV*, *12*.

T HE substance of this chapter is this, that what is intended by the Day of Resurrection is the Day of the appearance of the Tree of divine Reality, but it is not seen that any one of the followers of Shí'ih Islám hath understood the meaning of the Day of Resurrection; rather have they fancifully imagined a thing which with God hath no reality. In the estimation of God and according to the usage of such as are initiated into divine mysteries, what is meant by the Day of Resurrection is this, that from the time of the appearance of Him Who is the Tree of divine Reality, at whatever period and under whatever name, until the

moment of His disappearance, is the Day of Resurrection.
For example, from the inception of the mission of Jesus
—may peace be upon Him—till the day of His ascension
was the Resurrection of Moses. For during that period the
Revelation of God shone forth through the appearance of
that divine Reality, Who rewarded by His Word everyone
who believed in Moses, and punished by His Word everyone who did not believe; inasmuch as God's Testimony for
that Day was that which He had solemnly affirmed in the
Gospel. And from the inception of the Revelation of the
Apostle of God—may the blessings of God be upon Him—
till the day of His ascension was the Resurrection of Jesus—
peace be upon Him—wherein the Tree of divine Reality
appeared in the person of Muḥammad, rewarding by His
Word everyone who was a believer in Jesus, and punishing
by His Word everyone who was not a believer in Him.
And from the moment when the Tree of the Bayán
appeared until it disappeareth is the Resurrection of the
Apostle of God, as is divinely foretold in the Qur'án; the
beginning of which was when two hours and eleven
minutes had passed on the eve of the fifth of Jamádíyu'l-
Avval, 1260 A.H.,[1] which is the year 1270 of the Declaration of the Mission of Muḥammad. This was the beginning
of the Day of Resurrection of the Qur'án, and until the
disappearance of the Tree of divine Reality is the Resurrection of the Qur'án. The stage of perfection of everything is
reached when its resurrection occurreth. The perfection of
the religion of Islám was consummated at the beginning
of this Revelation; and from the rise of this Revelation until
its setting, the fruits of the Tree of Islám, whatever they
are, will become apparent. The Resurrection of the Bayán
will occur at the time of the appearance of Him Whom

[1] 22 May 1844

God shall make manifest. For today the Bayán is in the stage of seed; at the beginning of the manifestation of Him Whom God shall make manifest its ultimate perfection will become apparent. He is made manifest in order to gather the fruits of the trees He hath planted; even as the Revelation of the Qá'im [He Who ariseth], a descendant of Muḥammad—may the blessings of God rest upon Him— is exactly like unto the Revelation of the Apostle of God Himself [Muḥammad]. He appeareth not, save for the purpose of gathering the fruits of Islám from the Qur'ánic verses which He [Muḥammad] hath sown in the hearts of men. The fruits of Islám cannot be gathered except through allegiance unto Him [the Qá'im] and by believing in Him. At the present time, however, only adverse effects have resulted; for although He hath appeared in the midmost heart of Islám, and all people profess it by reason of their relationship to Him [the Qá'im], yet unjustly have they consigned Him to the Mountain of Mákú, and this notwithstanding that in the Qur'án the advent of the Day of Resurrection hath been promised unto all by God. For on that Day all men will be brought before God and will attain His Presence; which meaneth appearance before Him Who is the Tree of divine Reality and attainment unto His presence; inasmuch as it is not possible to appear before the Most Holy Essence of God, nor is it conceivable to seek reunion with Him. That which is feasible in the matter of appearance before Him and of meeting Him is attainment unto the Primal Tree. *II, 7.*

THE evidence set forth by God can never be compared with the evidences produced by any one of the peoples and kindreds of the earth; and beyond a shadow of doubt no evidence is set forth by God save through the One Who is appointed as His supreme Testimony. Moreover, the proof of revealed verses doth, alone and of itself, conclusively demonstrate the utter impotence of all created things on earth, for this is a proof which hath proceeded from God and shall endure until the Day of Resurrection.

And if anyone should reflect on the appearance of this Tree, he will undoubtedly testify to the loftiness of the Cause of God. For if one from whose life only twenty-four years have passed, and who is devoid of those sciences wherein all are learned, now reciteth verses after such fashion without thought or hesitation, writes a thousand verses of prayer in the course of five hours without pause of the pen, and produceth commentaries and learned treatises on such lofty themes as the true understanding of God and of the oneness of His Being, in a manner which doctors and philosophers confess surpasseth their power of understanding, then there is no doubt that all that hath been manifested is divinely inspired. Notwithstanding their life-long diligent study, what pains do these divines take when writing a single line in Arabic! Yet after such efforts the result is but words which are unworthy of mention. All these things are for a proof unto the people; otherwise the religion of God is too mighty and glorious for anyone to comprehend through aught but itself; rather by it all else is understood. *II, 1.*

PRAISE be to God that He hath enabled us to become cognizant of Him Whom God shall make manifest in the Day of Resurrection, so that we may derive benefit from the fruit of our existence and be not deprived of attaining the presence of God. For indeed this is the object of our creation and the sole purpose underlying every virtuous deed we may perform. Such is the bounty which God hath conferred upon us; verily He is the All-Bountiful, the Gracious. Know thou, that thou wilt succeed in doing so if thou believest with undoubting faith. However, since thou canst not attain the state of undoubting faith, due to the intervening veils of thy selfish desires, therefore thou wilt tarry in the fire, though realizing it not. On the Day of His manifestation, unless thou truly believest in Him, naught can save thee from the fire, even if thou dost perform every righteous deed. If thou embracest the Truth, everything good and seemly shall be set down for thee in the Book of God, and by virtue of this thou wilt rejoice in the all-highest Paradise until the following Resurrection.

Consider with due attention, for the path is very strait, even while it is more spacious than the heavens and the earth and what is between them. For instance, if all those who were expecting the fulfilment of the promise of Jesus had been assured of the manifestation of Muḥammad, the Apostle of God, not one would have turned aside from the sayings of Jesus. So likewise in the Revelation of the Point of the Bayán, if all should be assured that this is that same Promised Mihdí [One Who is guided] whom the Apostle of God foretold, not one of the believers in the Qur'án would turn aside from the sayings of the Apostle of God. So likewise in the Revelation of Him Whom God shall make manifest, behold the same thing; for should all be assured that He is that same 'He Whom God shall make manifest' whom the Point of the Bayán hath foretold, not one would turn aside. *IX, 3.*

In the Name of God, the Most Exalted, the Most Holy. All praise and glory befitteth the sacred and glorious court of the sovereign Lord, Who from everlasting hath dwelt, and unto everlasting will continue to dwell within the mystery of His Own divine Essence, Who from time immemorial hath abided and will forever continue to abide within His transcendent eternity, exalted above the reach and ken of all created beings. The sign of His matchless Revelation as created by Him and imprinted upon the realities of all beings, is none other but their powerlessness to know Him. The light He hath shed upon all things is none but the splendour of His Own Self. He Himself hath at all times been immeasurably exalted above any association with His creatures. He hath fashioned the entire creation in such wise that all beings may, by virtue of their innate powers, bear witness before God on the Day of Resurrection that He hath no peer or equal and is sanctified from any likeness, similitude or comparison. He hath been and will ever be one and incomparable in the transcendent glory of His divine being and He hath ever been indescribably mighty in the sublimity of His sovereign Lordship. No one hath ever been able befittingly to recognize Him nor will any man succeed at any time in comprehending Him as is truly meet and seemly, for any reality to which the term 'being' is applicable hath been created by the sovereign Will of the Almighty, Who hath shed upon it the radiance of His Own Self, shining forth from His most august station. He hath moreover deposited within the realities of all created things the emblem of His recognition, that everyone may know of a certainty that He is the Beginning and the End, the Manifest and the Hidden, the Maker and the Sustainer, the Omnipotent and the All-Knowing, the One Who heareth and perceiveth all things, He Who is invincible in His power and standeth supreme in His Own identity, He Who quickeneth and causeth to die, the All-Powerful, the Inaccessible, the Most Exalted, the Most High. Every revelation of His divine Essence betokens the sublimity of His glory, the loftiness of His sanctity, the inaccessible height of His oneness and the exaltation of His majesty and power. His beginning hath had no beginning other than His Own firstness and His end knoweth no end save His Own lastness. *I, 1.*

THE revelation of the Divine Reality hath everlastingly been identical with its concealment and its concealment identical with its revelation. That which is intended by 'Revelation of God' is the Tree of divine Truth that betokeneth none but Him, and it is this divine Tree that hath raised and will raise up Messengers, and hath revealed and will ever reveal Scriptures. From eternity unto eternity this Tree of divine Truth hath served and will ever serve as the throne of the revelation and concealment of God among His creatures, and in every age is made manifest through whomsoever He pleaseth. At the time of the revelation of the Qur'án He asserted His transcendent power through the advent of Muḥammad, and on the occasion of the revelation of the Bayán He demonstrated His sovereign might through the appearance of the Point of the Bayán, and when Him Whom God shall make manifest will shine forth, it will be through Him that He will vindicate the truth of His Faith, as He pleaseth, with whatsoever He pleaseth and for whatsoever He pleaseth. He is with all things, yet nothing is with Him. He is not within a thing nor above it nor beside it. Any reference to His being established upon the throne implieth that the Exponent of His Revelation is established upon the seat of transcendent authority . . .

He hath everlastingly existed and will everlastingly continue to exist. He hath been and will ever remain inscrutable unto all men, inasmuch as all else besides Him have been and shall ever be created through the potency of His command. He is exalted above every mention or praise and is sanctified beyond every word of commendation or every comparison. No created thing comprehendeth Him, while He in truth comprehendeth all things. Even when it is said 'no created thing comprehendeth Him', this refers to the Mirror of His Revelation, that is Him Whom God shall make manifest. Indeed too high and exalted is He for anyone to allude unto Him. *II, 8.*

4

EXCERPTS FROM DALÁ'IL-I-SAB'IH

(The Seven Proofs)

THOU hast asked concerning the fundamentals of religion and its ordinances: Know thou that first and foremost in religion is the knowledge of God. This attaineth its consummation in the recognition of His divine unity, which in turn reacheth its fulfilment in acclaiming that His hallowed and exalted Sanctuary, the Seat of His transcendent majesty, is sanctified from all attributes. And know thou that in this world of being the knowledge of God can never be attained save through the knowledge of Him Who is the Dayspring of divine Reality.

GRACIOUS God! Within the domains of Islám there are at present seven powerful sovereigns ruling the world. None of them hath been informed of His [the Báb's] Manifestation, and if informed, none hath believed in Him. Who knoweth, they may leave this world below full of desire, and without having realized that the thing for which they were waiting had come to pass. This is what happened to the monarchs that held fast unto the Gospel. They awaited the coming of the Prophet of God [Muḥammad], and when He did appear, they failed to recognize Him. Behold how great are the sums which these sovereigns expend without even the slightest thought of appointing an official charged with the task of acquainting them in their own realms with the Manifestation of God! They would thereby have fulfilled the purpose for which they have been created. All their desires have been and are still fixed upon leaving behind them traces of their names.

PONDER likewise the Dispensation of the Apostle of God which lasted twelve hundred and seventy years[1] till the dawn of the manifestation of the Bayán. He directed everyone to await the advent of the Promised Qá'im. All deeds which in the Islamic Dispensation began with Muḥammad should find their consummation through the appearance of the Qá'im. God hath made Him manifest invested with the proof wherewith the Apostle of God was invested, so that none of the believers in the Qur'án might entertain doubts about the validity of His Cause, for it is set down in the Qur'án that none but God is capable of revealing verses. During the period of 1270 years no one among the followers of the Qur'án ever witnessed a person appearing with conclusive proofs. Now the Ever-Living Lord hath made manifest and invested with supreme testimony this long-awaited Promised One from a place no one could imagine and from a person whose knowledge was deemed of no account. His age is no more than twenty-five years, yet His glory is such as none of the learned among the people of Islám can rival; inasmuch as man's glory lieth in his knowledge. Behold the learned who are honoured by virtue of their ability to understand the Holy Writings, and God hath exalted them to such a degree that in referring to them He saith: 'None knoweth the meaning thereof except God and them that are well-grounded in knowledge.'[2] How strange then that this twenty-five-year-old untutored one should be singled out to reveal His verses in so astounding a manner. If the Muslim divines have cause for pride in understanding the meaning of the Holy

[1] From the Declaration of Muḥammad; this occurred ten years before the Hijrah which marks the starting point of the Muslim calendar.

[2] Qur'án 3:5

Writings, His glory is in revealing the Writings, that none of them may hesitate to believe in His Words. So great is the celestial might and power which God hath revealed in Him that if it were His will and no break should intervene He could, within the space of five days and nights, reveal the equivalent of the Qur'án which was sent down in twenty-three years. Ponder thou and reflect. Hath anyone like unto Him ever appeared in former times, or is this characteristic strictly confined unto Him?

CONSIDER the manifold favours vouchsafed by the Promised One, and the effusions of His bounty which have pervaded the concourse of the followers of Islám to enable them to attain unto salvation. Indeed observe how He Who representeth the origin of creation, He Who is the Exponent of the verse, 'I, in very truth, am God', identified Himself as the Gate [Báb] for the advent of the promised Qá'im, a descendant of Muḥammad, and in His first Book enjoined the observance of the laws of the Qur'án, so that the people might not be seized with perturbation by reason of a new Book and a new Revelation and might regard His Faith as similar to their own, perchance they would not turn away from the Truth and ignore the thing for which they had been called into being.

LET Me set forth some rational arguments for thee. If someone desireth to embrace the Faith of Islám today, would the testimony of God prove conclusive for him? If thou dost contend that it would not, then how is it that God will chastise him after death, and that, while he lives, the verdict of 'non-believer' is passed upon him? If thou affirmest that the testimony is conclusive, how wouldst thou prove this? If thy assertion is based on hearsay, then mere words are unacceptable as a binding testimony; but if thou deemest the Qur'án as the testimony, this would be a weighty and evident proof.

Now consider the Revelation of the Bayán. If the followers of the Qur'án had applied to themselves proofs similar to those which they advance for the non-believers in Islám, not a single soul would have remained deprived of the Truth, and on the Day of Resurrection everyone would have attained salvation.

Should a Christian contend, 'How can I deem the Qur'án a testimony while I am unable to understand it?' such a contention would not be acceptable. Likewise the people of the Qur'án disdainfully observe, 'We are unable to comprehend the eloquence of the verses in the Bayán, how can we regard it as a testimony?' Whoever uttereth such words, say unto him, 'O thou untutored one! By what proof hast thou embraced the Religion of Islám? Is it the Prophet on whom thou hast never set eyes? Is it the miracles which thou hast never witnessed? If thou hast accepted Islám unwittingly, wherefore hast thou done so? But if thou hast embraced the Faith by recognizing the Qur'án as the testimony, because thou hast heard the learned and the faithful express their powerlessness before it, or if thou hast, upon hearing the divine verses and by virtue of thy spontaneous love for the True Word of God, responded in a spirit of utter humility and lowliness—a spirit which is one of the mightiest signs of true love and understanding—then such proofs have been and will ever be regarded as sound.'

THE recognition of Him Who is the Bearer of divine Truth is none other than the recognition of God, and loving Him is none other than loving God. However, I swear by the sublime Essence of God—exalted and glorified be He—that I did not wish my identity to be known by men, and gave instructions that My name should be concealed, because I was fully aware of the incapacity of this people, who are none other than those who have, in reference to no less a person than the Apostle of God—incomparable as He hath ever been—remarked, 'He is certainly a lunatic'.[1] If they now claim to be other than those people, their deeds bear witness to the falsity of their assertions. That which God testifieth is none other than what His supreme Testimony testifieth. Were all the peoples of the world to testify unto a thing and were He to testify unto another, His testimony will be regarded as God's testimony, while aught else but Him hath been and will ever be as naught; for it is through His might that a thing assumeth existence.

Consider the extent of the adherence of these people to matters of faith. When dealing with their own affairs they are well content with the testimony of two just witnesses, and yet despite the testimony of so many righteous men they hesitate to believe in Him Who is the Bearer of the divine Truth.

THE evidences which the people demanded from the Apostle of God through their idle fancy have mostly been rejected in the Qur'án, even as in the Súrih of the Children

[1] Qur'án 68:51

of Israel [Súrih xvii] it hath been revealed: 'And they say, by no means will we believe on thee till thou cause a fountain to gush forth for us from the earth; or till thou have a garden of palm trees and vines, and thou cause rivers to spring forth from the midst thereof in abundance; or thou cause the heaven to fall down upon us, as thou hast given out, in pieces; or thou bring God and the angels to vouch for thee; or thou have a house of gold; or thou ascend to heaven nor will we believe in thine ascension, till thou send down to us a book which we may read. Say, Praise be to my Lord! Am I more than a man, an apostle?'

Now be fair! The Arabs uttered such words, and now, prompted by thy desire, thou dost demand yet other things? What is the difference between thee and them? If thou dost ponder a while, it will be evident that it is incumbent upon a lowly servant to acquiesce to whatever proof God hath appointed, and not to follow his own idle fancy. If the wishes of the people were to be gratified not a single disbeliever would remain on earth. For once the Apostle of God had fulfilled the wishes of the people they would unhesitatingly have embraced His Faith. May God save thee, shouldst thou seek any evidence according to thy selfish desire; rather it behooveth thee to uphold the unfailing proof which God hath appointed. The object of thy belief in God is but to secure His good-pleasure. How then dost thou seek as a proof of thy faith a thing which hath been and is contrary to His good-pleasure?

Rid thou thyself of all attachments to aught except God, enrich thyself in God by dispensing with all else besides Him, and recite this prayer:

Say: God sufficeth all things above all things, and nothing in the heavens or in the earth or in whatever lieth between them but God, thy Lord, sufficeth. Verily, He is in Himself the Knower, the Sustainer, the Omnipotent.

Regard not the all-sufficing power of God as an idle fancy. It is that genuine faith which thou cherishest for the Manifestation of God in every Dispensation. It is such faith which sufficeth above all the things that exist on the earth, whereas no created thing on earth besides faith would suffice thee. If thou art not a believer, the Tree of divine Truth would condemn thee to extinction. If thou art a believer, thy faith shall be sufficient for thee above all things that exist on earth, even though thou possess nothing.

It is recorded in a tradition that of the entire concourse of the Christians no more than seventy people embraced the Faith of the Apostle of God. The blame falleth upon their doctors, for if these had believed, they would have been followed by the mass of their countrymen. Behold, then, that which hath come to pass! The learned men of Christendom are held to be learned by virtue of their safeguarding the teaching of Christ, and yet consider how they themselves have been the cause of men's failure to accept the Faith and attain unto salvation! Is it still thy wish to follow in their footsteps? The followers of Jesus submitted to their clerics to be saved on the Day of Resurrection, and as a result of this obedience they eventually entered into the fire, and on the Day when the Apostle of God appeared they shut themselves out from the recognition of His exalted Person. Dost thou desire to follow such divines?

Nay, by God, be thou neither a divine without discernment nor a follower without discernment, for both of these shall perish on the Day of Resurrection. Rather it behooveth thee to be a discerning divine, or to walk with insight in the way of God by obeying a true leader of religion.

In every nation thou beholdest unnumbered spiritual leaders who are bereft of true discernment, and among every people thou dost encounter myriads of adherents who are devoid of the same characteristic. Ponder for a while in thy heart, have pity on thyself and turn not aside thine attention from proofs and evidences. However, seek not proofs and evidences after thine idle fancy; but rather base thy proofs upon what God hath appointed. Moreover, know thou that neither being a man of learning nor being a follower is in itself a source of glory. If thou art a man of learning, thy knowledge becometh an honour, and if thou art a follower, thine adherence unto leadership becometh an honour, only when these conform to the good-pleasure of God. And beware lest thou regard as an idle fancy the good-pleasure of God; it is the same as the good-pleasure of His Messenger. Consider the followers of Jesus. They were eagerly seeking the good-pleasure of God, yet none of them attained the good-pleasure of His Apostle which is identical with God's good-pleasure, except such as embraced His Faith.

Thy letter hath been perused. Were the truth of this Revelation to be fully demonstrated with elaborate proofs, all the scrolls that exist in the heaven and on the earth would be insufficient to contain them.

However, the substance and essence of the subject is this, that there can be no doubt that from everlasting God hath been invested with the independent sovereignty of His exalted Being, and unto everlasting He will remain inaccessible in the transcendent majesty of His holy Essence. No creature hath ever recognized Him as befitteth His recognition, nor hath any created being ever praised Him as is worthy of His praise. He is exalted above every name, and is sanctified from every comparison. Through Him all things are made known, while too lofty is His reality to be known through anyone but Him. The process of His creation hath had no beginning and can have no end, otherwise it would necessitate the cessation of His celestial grace. God hath raised up Prophets and revealed Books as numerous as the creatures of the world, and will continue to do so to everlasting.

If thou art sailing upon the sea of God's Names, which are reflected in all things, know thou that He is exalted and sanctified from being known through His creatures, or being described by His servants. Everything thou beholdest hath been called into being through the operation of His Will. How can such a created thing, therefore, be indicative of His essential oneness? God's existence in itself testifieth to His Own oneness, while every created thing, by its very nature, beareth evidence that it hath been fashioned by God. Such is the proof of consummate wisdom in the estimation of those who sail the ocean of divine Truth.

If, however, thou art sailing upon the sea of creation,

know thou that the First Remembrance, which is the Primal Will of God, may be likened unto the sun. God hath created Him through the potency of His might, and He hath, from the beginning that hath no beginning, caused Him to be manifested in every Dispensation through the compelling power of His behest, and God will, to the end that knoweth no end, continue to manifest Him according to the good-pleasure of His invincible Purpose.

And know thou that He indeed resembleth the sun. Were the risings of the sun to continue till the end that hath no end, yet there hath not been nor ever will be more than one sun; and were its settings to endure for evermore, still there hath not been nor ever will be more than one sun. It is this Primal Will which appeareth resplendent in every Prophet and speaketh forth in every revealed Book. It knoweth no beginning, inasmuch as the First deriveth its firstness from It; and knoweth no end, for the Last oweth its lastness unto It.

In the time of the First Manifestation the Primal Will appeared in Adam; in the day of Noah It became known in Noah; in the day of Abraham in Him; and so in the day of Moses; the day of Jesus; the day of Muḥammad, the Apostle of God; the day of the 'Point of the Bayán'; the day of Him Whom God shall make manifest; and the day of the One Who will appear after Him Whom God shall make manifest. Hence the inner meaning of the words uttered by the Apostle of God, 'I am all the Prophets', inasmuch as what shineth resplendent in each one of Them hath been and will ever remain the one and the same sun.

5

EXCERPTS FROM THE KITÁB-I-ASMÁ'

(The Book of Names)

ye that are invested with the Bayán! Denounce ye not one another, ere the Day-Star of ancient eternity shineth forth above the horizon of His sublimity. We have created you from one tree and have caused you to be as the leaves and fruit of the same tree, that haply ye may become a source of comfort to one another. Regard ye not others save as ye regard your own selves, that no feeling of aversion may prevail amongst you so as to shut you out from Him Whom God shall make manifest on the Day of Resurrection. It behooveth you all to be one indivisible people; thus should ye return unto Him Whom God shall make manifest.

Those who have deprived themselves of this Resurrection by reason of their mutual hatreds or by regarding themselves to be in the right and others in the wrong, were chastised on the Day of Resurrection by reason of such hatreds evinced during their night.[1] Thus they deprived themselves of beholding the countenance of God, and this for no other reason than mutual denunciations.

O ye that are invested with the Bayán! Ye should perform such deeds as would please God, your Lord, earning thereby the good-pleasure of Him Whom God shall make manifest. Turn not your religion into a means of material

---

[1] By 'night' is meant the period between two divine Revelations when the Sun of Truth is not manifest among men. In the Persian Bayán, *II, 7*, the Báb says, 'O people of the Bayán! Act not as the people of the Qur'án have acted, for if you do so the fruits of your night will come to naught'.

gain, spending your life on vanities, and inheriting thereby on the Day of Resurrection that which would displease Him Whom God shall make manifest, while ye deem that what ye do is right. If, however, ye observe piety in your Faith, God will surely nourish you from the treasuries of His heavenly grace.

Be ye sincere in your allegiance to Him Whom God shall make manifest, for the sake of God, your Lord, that perchance ye may, through devotion to His Faith, be redeemed on the Day of Resurrection. Beware lest ye suffer one another to be wrapt in veils by reason of the disputes which may, during your night, arise among you as a result of the problems ye encounter or in consideration of such matters as your loftiness or lowliness, your nearness or remoteness.

Thus have We firmly exhorted you—a befitting exhortation indeed—that haply ye may cleave tenaciously unto it and attain thereby salvation on the Day of Resurrection. The time is approaching when ye will be at peace with yourselves in your homes, and lo, Him Whom God shall make manifest will have appeared, and God wisheth you to return unto Him, even as God called you into being through the Primal Point. However, all of you will seek guidance while pursuing the promptings of your own desires. Some of you are filled with pride by reason of your religion, others because of your learning. Ye will, one and all, cling unto some part of the Bayán as a means of self-glorification. *XVI, 19*.[1]

[1] The Kitáb-i-Asmá' is divided into váḥids and chapters, to which these numbers refer.

God is sanctified from His servants and no direct relationship ever existeth between Him and any created thing,
while ye have all arisen at His bidding. Verily He is your
Lord and your God, your Master and your King. He
ordaineth your movements at His behest throughout the
day-time and in the night season.

Say, He Whom God shall make manifest is indeed the
Primal Veil of God. Above this Veil ye can find nothing
other than God, while beneath it ye can discern all things
emanating from God. He is the Unseen, the Inaccessible,
the Most Exalted, the Best Beloved.

If ye seek God, it behooveth you to seek Him Whom
God shall make manifest, and if ye cherish the desire to
dwell in the Ark of Names, ye will be distinguished as the
guides to Him Whom God shall make manifest, did ye but
believe in Him. Verily then make your hearts the day-
springs of His exalted Names as recorded in the Book, and
ye shall, even as mirrors placed before the sun, be able to
receive enlightenment. *XVI, 17.*

Should a person lay claim to a cause and produce his
proofs, then those who seek to repudiate him are required
to produce proofs like unto his. If they succeed in doing so,
his words will prove vain and they will prevail; otherwise
neither his words will cease nor the proofs he hath set forth
will become void. I admonish you, O ye who are invested
with the Bayán, if ye would fain assert your ascendancy,
confront not any soul unless ye give proofs similar to that
which he hath adduced; for Truth shall be firmly established, while aught else besides it is sure to perish.

How numerous the people who engaged in contests with Muḥammad, the Apostle of God, and were eventually reduced to naught, inasmuch as they were powerless to bring forth proofs similar to that which God had sent down unto Him. Had they been abashed and modest, and had they realized the nature of the proofs wherewith He was invested, they would never have challenged Him. But they regarded themselves as champions of their own religion. Therefore God laid hold on them according to their deserts and vindicated the Truth through the power of Truth. This is what ye clearly perceive today in the Muḥammadan Revelation.

Who is the man amongst you who can challenge the exalted Thrones of Reality in every Dispensation, while all existence is wholly dependent upon Them? Indeed, God hath wiped out all those who have opposed Them from the beginning that hath no beginning until the present day and hath conclusively demonstrated the Truth through the power of Truth. Verily, He is the Almighty, the Omnipotent, the All-Powerful. *XVII, 11.*

O YE who are invested with the Bayán! Be ye watchful on the Day of Resurrection, for on that Day ye will firmly believe in the Váḥid of the Bayán, though this, even as your past religion which proved of no avail, can in no wise benefit you, unless ye embrace the Cause of Him Whom God shall make manifest and believe in that which He ordaineth. Therefore take ye good heed lest ye shut yourselves out from Him Who is the Fountain-head of all Messengers and Scriptures, while ye hold fast to parts

of the teachings which have emanated from these sources.
XVII, 15.

Consider how at the time of the appearance of every
Revelation, those who open their hearts to the Author of
that Revelation recognize the Truth, while the hearts of
those who fail to apprehend the Truth are straitened by
reason of their shutting themselves out from Him. However, openness of heart is bestowed by God upon both
parties alike. God desireth not to straiten the heart of
anyone, be it even an ant, how much less the heart of a
superior creature, except when he suffereth himself to be
wrapt in veils, for God is the Creator of all things.

Wert thou to open the heart of a single soul by helping
him to embrace the Cause of Him Whom God shall make
manifest, thine inmost being would be filled with the in-
spirations of that august Name. It devolveth upon you,
therefore, to perform this task in the Days of Resurrection,
inasmuch as most people are helpless, and wert thou to
open their hearts and dispel their doubts, they would gain
admittance into the Faith of God. Therefore, manifest thou
this attribute to the utmost of thine ability in the days of
Him Whom God shall make manifest. For indeed if thou
dost open the heart of a person for His sake, better will it
be for thee than every virtuous deed; since deeds are
secondary to faith in Him and certitude in His Reality.
XVII, 15.

Take heed to carefully consider the words of every soul, then hold fast to the proofs which attest the truth. If ye fail to discover truth in a person's words, make them not the object of contention, inasmuch as ye have been forbidden in the Bayán to enter into idle disputation and controversy, that perchance on the Day of Resurrection ye may not engage in argumentation, and dispute with Him Whom God shall make manifest. *XVII, 16.*

On the Day of Resurrection when He Whom God will make manifest cometh unto you, invested with conclusive proofs, ye shall hold His Cause as being devoid of truth, whereas God hath apprised you in the Bayán that no similarity existeth between the Cause of Him Whom God will make manifest and the cause of others. How can anyone besides God reveal a verse such as to overwhelm all mankind? Say, great is God! Who else but Him Whom God will make manifest can spontaneously recite verses which proceed from His Lord—a feat that no mortal man can ever hope to accomplish?

Truth can in no wise be confounded with aught else except itself; would that ye might ponder His proof. Nor can error be confused with Truth, if ye do but reflect upon the testimony of God, the True One.

How great hath been the number of those who have falsely laid claim to a cause within Islám, and ye followed in their footsteps without having witnessed a single proof. What evidence can ye then produce in the presence of your Lord, if ye do but meditate a while?

Take ye good heed in your night[1] lest ye be a cause of

1 See footnote on page 129

sadness to any soul, whether ye be able to discover proofs in him or not, that haply on the Day of Resurrection ye may not grieve Him within Whose grasp lieth every proof. And when ye do not discern God's testimony in a person, he will verily fail in manifesting the power of Truth; and God is sufficient to deal with him. Indeed on no account should ye sadden any person; surely God will put him to the proof and bring him to account. It behooveth you to cling to the testimony of your own Faith and to observe the ordinances laid down in the Bayán.

You are like unto the man who layeth out an orchard and planteth all kinds of fruit trees therein. When the time is at hand for him, the lord, to come, ye will have taken possession of the orchard in his name, and when he doth come in person, ye will shut him out from it.

Verily We planted the Tree of the Qur'án and provided its Orchard with all kinds of fruit, whereof ye all have been partaking. Then when We came to take over that which We had planted, ye pretended not to know Him Who is the Lord thereof.

Be ye not a cause of grief unto Us, nor withhold Us from this Orchard which belongeth unto Us, though independent are We of all that ye possess. Moreover, unto none of you shall We make this property lawful, were it even to the extent of a mustard seed. Verily, the Reckoner are We.

We have planted the Garden of the Bayán in the name of Him Whom God will make manifest, and have granted you permission to live therein until the time of His manifestation; then from the moment the Cause of Him Whom God will make manifest is inaugurated, We forbid you all the things ye hold as your own, unless ye may, by the leave of your Lord, be able to regain possession thereof. *XVIII, 3.*

O YE unto whom the Bayán is given! Be ye vigilant lest in the days of Him Whom God shall make manifest, while ye consider yourselves as seeking God's pleasure, in reality ye persist in that which would only displease Him, even as did those who lived in the days of the Primal Point, to whom it never occurred that they were seeking things which ran counter to that which God had purposed. They shut themselves out as by a veil from God and failed to observe that which He had desired for them to perform as true believers. They pondered not upon such people as lived in the days of Muḥammad, who believed likewise that they were seeking the good-pleasure of God, while they had actually cut themselves off therefrom, once they had failed to secure the good-pleasure of Muḥammad. Nevertheless they comprehended not.

O ye who are invested with the Bayán! Regard not yourselves as being like unto the people to whom the Qur'án or the Gospel or other Scriptures of old were given, since at the time of His manifestation ye shall stray farther from God than did they. If ye happen to shut yourselves out it would never cross your minds that ye were shut out from Him. It behooveth you to consider how the people unto whom the Qur'án was given were debarred from the Truth, for indeed ye will act in a like manner, thinking that ye are doers of good. If ye perceive the degree of your deprivation of God, ye will wish to have perished from the face of the earth and to have sunk into oblivion. The day will come when ye will earnestly desire to know that which would meet with the good-pleasure of God but, alas, ye shall find no path unto Him. Ye, even as camels that wander aimlessly, will not find a pasture wherein ye may gather and unite upon a Cause in which ye can assuredly believe. At that time God shall cause the Sun of Truth to shine forth and the oceans of His bounty and grace to surge, while ye will have chosen droplets of water as the object of your desire, and will have deprived yourselves of the plenteous waters in His oceans.

If ye entertain any doubts in this matter consider the people unto whom the Gospel was given. Having no access to the apostles of Jesus, they sought the pleasure of the Lord in their churches, hoping to learn that which would be acceptable unto God, but they found therein no path unto Him. Then when God manifested Muḥammad as His Messenger and as the Repository of His good-pleasure, they neglected to quicken their souls from the Fountain of living waters which streamed forth from the presence of their Lord and continued to rove distraught upon the earth seeking a mere droplet of water and believing that they were doing righteous deeds. They behaved as the people unto whom the Qur'án was given are now behaving.

O ye who are invested with the Bayán! Ye can act similarly. Take ye heed, therefore, lest ye deprive yourselves of attaining the presence of Him Who is the Manifestation of God, notwithstanding that ye have been day and night praying to behold His countenance; and be ye careful lest ye be deterred from attaining unto the ocean of His good-pleasure, when perplexed and to no avail ye roam the earth in search of a drop of water.

Say, the testimony of God hath been fulfilled in the Bayán, and through its revelation the grace of God hath attained its highest consummation for all mankind. Let no one among you say that God hath withheld the outpouring of His bounty unto you, for assuredly God's mercy unto those to whom the Bayán is given hath been fulfilled and completed until the Day of Resurrection. Would that ye might believe in the signs of God. *XVI, 13.*

VERILY God hath caused the people of the Bayán to be called into being through the power of Him unto Whom the Bayán was revealed, in preparation for the Day when they will return to their Lord.

Indeed those who will bear allegiance unto Him Whom God shall make manifest are the ones who have grasped the meaning of that which hath been revealed in the Bayán; they are indeed the sincere ones, while those who turn away from Him at the time of His appearance will have utterly failed to comprehend a single letter of the Bayán, even though they profess belief and assurance in whatever is revealed in it or observe its precepts.

Say, every favourable and praiseworthy designation in the Bayán is but an allusion to those who recognize Him Whom God shall make manifest, and who believe with certainty in God and in His holy Writings, while every unfavourable designation therein is meant to refer to such as repudiate Him Whom God shall make manifest, though they may act uprightly within the bounds laid down in the Bayán. Say, if ye embrace the truth on the Day of Resurrection, God will assuredly pardon you for your night[1] and will grant you forgiveness.

As to those who have faithfully observed the ordinances in the Bayán from the inception of its revelation until the Day when Him Whom God shall make manifest will appear, these are indeed the companions of the paradise of His good-pleasure who will be glorified in the presence of God and will dwell in the pavilions of His celestial Garden. Yet, within less than a tiny fraction of an instant from the moment God will have revealed Him Who is the Manifestation of His Own Self, the entire company of the followers of the Bayán shall be put to proof. *XVII, 1.*

[1] See footnote on page 129

SINCE thou hast faithfully obeyed the true religion of God in the past, it behooveth thee to follow His true religion hereafter, inasmuch as every religion proceedeth from God, the Help in Peril, the Self-Subsisting.

He Who hath revealed the Qur'án unto Muḥammad, the Apostle of God, ordaining in the Faith of Islám that which was pleasing unto Him, hath likewise revealed the Bayán, in the manner ye have been promised, unto Him Who is your Qá'im,[1] your Guide, your Mihdí,[2] your Lord, Him Whom ye acclaim as the manifestation of God's most excellent titles. Verily the equivalent of that which God revealed unto Muḥammad during twenty-three years, hath been revealed unto Me within the space of two days and two nights. However, as ordained by God, no distinction is to be drawn between the two. He, in truth, hath power over all things.

I swear by the life of Him Whom God shall make manifest! My Revelation is indeed far more bewildering than that of Muḥammad, the Apostle of God, if thou dost but pause to reflect upon the days of God. Behold, how strange that a person brought up amongst the people of Persia should be empowered by God to proclaim such irrefutable utterances as to silence every man of learning, and be enabled to spontaneously reveal verses far more rapidly than anyone could possibly set down in writing. Verily, no God is there but Him, the Help in Peril, the Self-Subsisting. *XVI, 18.*

[1] He Who ariseth (*God Passes By*, p. 57)
[2] One Who is guided (*God Passes By*, p. 58)

As to those who have debarred themselves from the Revelation of God, they have indeed failed to understand the significance of a single letter of the Qur'án, nor have they obtained the slightest notion of the Faith of Islám, otherwise they would not have turned away from God, Who hath brought them into being, Who hath nurtured them, hath caused them to die and hath proffered life unto them, by clinging to parts of their religion, thinking that they are doing righteous work for the sake of God.

How numerous the verses which have been revealed concerning the grievous tests ye shall experience on the Day of Judgement, yet it appeareth that ye have never perused them; and how vast the number of revealed traditions regarding the trials which will overtake you on the Day of Our Return, and yet ye seem never to have set your eyes upon them.

Ye spend all your days contriving forms and rules for the principles of your Faith, while that which profiteth you in all this is to comprehend the good-pleasure of your Lord and unitedly to become well-acquainted with His supreme Purpose.

God hath made His Own Self known unto you, but ye have failed to recognize Him; and the thing which will, on the Day of Judgement, turn you aside from God is the specious character of your deeds. Throughout your lives ye follow your religion in order to attract the good-pleasure of God, yet on the Last Day ye shut yourselves out from God and turn away from Him Who is your Promised One. *XVII, 2.*

O YE who are invested with the Bayán! Ye shall be put to proof, even as those unto whom the Qur'án was given. Have pity on yourselves, for ye shall witness the Day when God will have revealed Him Who is the Manifestation of His Own Self, invested with clear and irrefutable proofs, while ye will cling tenaciously to the words the Witnesses of the Bayán have uttered. On that Day ye will continue to rove distraught, even as camels, seeking a drop of the water of life. God will cause oceans of living water to stream forth from the presence of Him Whom God shall make manifest, while ye will refuse to quench your thirst therefrom, notwithstanding that ye regard yourselves as the God-fearing witnesses of your Faith. Nay, and yet again, nay! Ye will go astray far beyond the peoples unto whom the Gospel, or the Qur'án or any other Scripture was given. Take good heed to yourselves, inasmuch as the Cause of God will come upon you at a time when you will all be entreating and tearfully imploring God for the advent of the Day of His Manifestation; yet when He cometh ye will tarry and will fail to be of those who are well-assured in His Faith.

Beware lest ye grieve Him Who is the Supreme Manifestation of your Lord; verily, He can well afford to dispense with your allegiance unto Him. Be ye careful and bring not despondency upon any soul, for surely ye shall be put to proof. *XVII, 2.*

S AY, He Whom God shall make manifest will surely redeem the rights of those who truly believe in God and in His signs, for they are the ones who merit reward from His presence. Say, it is far from the glory of Him Whom God shall make manifest that anyone should in this wise make mention of His name, if ye ponder the Cause of God in your hearts. Say, He shall vindicate the Cause through the potency of His command and shall bring to naught all perversion of truth by virtue of His behest. Verily God is potent over all things.

If ye wish to distinguish truth from error, consider those who believe in Him Whom God shall make manifest and those who disbelieve Him at the time of His appearance. The former represent the essence of truth, as attested in the Book of God, while the latter the essence of error, as attested in that same Book. Fear ye God that ye may not identify yourselves with aught but the truth, inasmuch as ye have been exalted in the Bayán for being recognized as the bearers of the name of Him Who is the eternal Truth.

Say, were He Whom God shall make manifest to pronounce a pious and truthful follower of the Bayán as false, it is incumbent upon you to submit to His decree, as this hath been affirmed by God in the Bayán; verily God is able to convert light into fire whenever He pleaseth; surely He is potent over all things. And were He to declare a person whom ye regard alien to the truth as being akin thereto, err not by questioning His decision in your fancies, for He Who is the Sovereign Truth createth things through the power of His behest. Verily God transmuteth fire into light as He willeth, and indeed potent is He over all things. Consider ye how the truth shone forth as truth in the First Day and how error became manifest as error; so likewise shall ye distinguish them from each other on the Day of Resurrection. *XVII, 4.*

Ponder upon the people unto whom the Gospel was given. Their religious leaders were considered as the true Guides of the Gospel, yet when they shut themselves out from Muḥammad, the Apostle of God, they turned into guides of error, notwithstanding that all their lives they had faithfully observed the precepts of their religion in order to attain unto Paradise; then when God made Paradise known unto them, they would not enter therein. Those unto whom the Qur'án is given have wrought likewise. They performed their acts of devotion for the sake of God, hoping that He might enable them to join the righteous in Paradise. However, when the gates of Paradise were flung open to their faces, they declined to enter. They suffered themselves to enter into the fire, though they had been seeking refuge therefrom in God.

Say, verily, the criterion by which truth is distinguished from error shall not appear until the Day of Resurrection. This ye will know, if ye be of them that love the Truth. And ere the advent of the Day of Resurrection ye shall distinguish truth from aught else besides it according to that which hath been revealed in the Bayán.

How vast the number of people who will, on the Day of Resurrection, regard themselves to be in the right, while they shall be accounted as false through the dispensation of Providence, inasmuch as they will shut themselves out as by a veil from Him Whom God shall make manifest and refuse to bow down in adoration before Him Who, as divinely ordained in the Book, is the Object of their creation. *XVII, 4.*

Say, ye will be unable to recognize the One True God or to discern clearly the words of divine guidance, inasmuch as ye seek and tread a path other than His. Whenever ye learn that a new Cause hath appeared, ye must seek the presence of its author and must delve into his writings that haply ye may not be debarred from attaining unto Him Whom God shall make manifest at the hour of His manifestation. Wert thou to walk in the way of truth as handed down by them that are endowed with the knowledge of the inmost reality, God, thy Lord, will surely redeem thee on the Day of Resurrection. Verily He is potent over all things.

In the Bayán God hath forbidden everyone to pronounce judgement against any soul, lest he may pass sentence upon God, his Lord, while regarding himself to be of the righteous, inasmuch as no one knoweth how the Cause of God will begin or end.

O ye who are invested with the Bayán! Should ye be apprised of a person laying claim to a Cause and revealing verses which to outward seeming are unlikely to have been revealed by anyone else save God, the Help in Peril, the Self-Subsisting, do not pass sentence against him, lest ye may inadvertently pass sentence against Him Whom God shall make manifest. Say, He Whom God shall make manifest is but one of you; He will make Himself known unto you on the Day of Resurrection. Ye shall know God when the Manifestation of His Own Self is made known unto you, that perchance ye may not stray far from His Path.

Verily God will raise up Him Whom God shall make manifest, and after Him Whomsoever He willeth, even as He hath raised up prophets before the Point of the Bayán. He in truth hath power over all things. *XVII, 4.*

VERILY, on the First Day We flung open the gates of Paradise unto all the peoples of the world, and exclaimed: 'O all ye created things! Strive to gain admittance into Paradise, since ye have, during all your lives, held fast unto virtuous deeds in order to attain unto it.' Surely all men yearn to enter therein, but alas, they are unable to do so by reason of that which their hands have wrought. Shouldst thou, however, gain a true understanding of God in thine heart of hearts, ere He hath manifested Himself, thou wouldst be able to recognize Him, visible and resplendent, when He unveileth Himself before the eyes of all men. *XVII, 11.*

SAY, by reason of your remembering Him Whom God shall make manifest and by extolling His name, God will cause your hearts to be dilated with joy, and do ye not wish your hearts to be in such a blissful state? Indeed the hearts of them that truly believe in Him Whom God shall make manifest are vaster than the expanse of heaven and earth and whatever is between them. God hath left no hindrance in their hearts, were it but the size of a mustard seed. He will cheer their hearts, their spirits, their souls and their bodies and their days of prosperity or adversity, through the exaltation of the name of Him Who is the supreme Testimony of God and the promotion of the Word of Him Who is the Dayspring of the glory of their Creator.

Verily, these are souls who take delight in the remembrance of God, Who dilates their hearts through the effulgence of the light of knowledge and wisdom. They seek naught but God and are oft engaged in giving praise unto Him. They desire naught except whatever He desireth and stand ready to do His bidding. Their hearts are mirrors reflecting whatsoever He Whom God shall make manifest willeth. Thus God will cheer the hearts of those who truly believe in Him and in His signs and who are well assured of the life to come. Say, the life to come is none other than the days associated with the coming of Him Whom God will make manifest.

Reduce not the ordinances of God to fanciful imaginations of your own; rather observe all the things which God hath created at His behest with the eye of the spirit, even as ye see things with the eyes of your bodies. *XVII, 15.*

THE divine Revelation associated with the advent of Him Who is your promised Mihdí hath proved far more wondrous than the Revelation wherewith Muḥammad, the Apostle of God, was invested. Would that ye might ponder. Verily, God raised up Muḥammad, the Apostle of God, from among the people of Arabia after he had reached forty years of age—a fact which every one of you affirmeth and upholdeth—while your Redeemer was raised up by God at the age of twenty-four amidst people none of whom can speak or understand a single word of Arabic. Thus God layeth bare the glory of His Cause and demonstrateth the Truth through the potency of His revealed Word. He is indeed the Powerful, the Omnipotent, the Help in Peril, the Best Beloved. *XVII, 4.*

Say, verily God hath caused all created things to enter beneath the shade of the tree of affirmation, except those who are endowed with the faculty of understanding. Theirs is the choice either to believe in God their Lord, and put their whole trust in Him, or to shut themselves out from Him and refuse to believe with certitude in His signs. These two groups sail upon two seas: the sea of affirmation and the sea of negation.

They that truly believe in God and in His signs, and who in every Dispensation faithfully obey that which hath been revealed in the Book—such are indeed the ones whom God hath created from the fruits of the Paradise of His good-pleasure, and who are of the blissful. But they who turn away from God and His signs in each Dispensation, those are the ones who sail upon the sea of negation.

God hath, through the potency of His behest, ordained for Himself the task of ensuring the ascendancy of the sea of affirmation and of bringing to naught the sea of negation through the power of His might. He is in truth potent over all things.

Verily it is incumbent upon you to recognize your Lord at the time of His manifestation, that haply ye may not enter into negation, and that, ere a prophet is raised by God, ye may find yourselves securely established upon the sea of affirmation. For if a prophet cometh to you from God and ye fail to walk in His Way, God will, thereupon, transform your light into fire. Take heed then that perchance ye may, through the grace of God and His signs, be enabled to redeem your souls. *XVIII, 13.*

Say, God shall of a truth cause your hearts to be given to perversity if ye fail to recognize Him Whom God shall make manifest; but if ye do recognize Him God shall banish perversity from your hearts . . .

That day whereon ye were, by God's Will, initiated into the Bayán, did any of you know who were the Letters of the Living or the Witnesses or the Testimonies or what the names of the believers? Likewise doth God wish you to recognize Him Whom God shall make manifest on the Day of Resurrection. Beware lest ye shut yourselves out as by a veil from Him Who hath created you, by reason of your regard for those who were called into being at the bidding of the Point of the Bayán for the exaltation of His Word. Did ye possess, ere the Point of the Bayán had called you into existence, any trace of identity, how much less a writ or authority? Disregard then your beginnings, perchance ye may be saved on the day of your return. Indeed had it not been for the exaltation of the name of the Primal Point, God would not have ordained for you the Letters of the Living, nor those who are the Testimonies of His Truth, nor the Witnesses of His Justice; could ye but heed a little. All this is to glorify the Cause of Him Whom God shall make manifest at the time of His manifestation; would that ye might ponder a while.

Therefore it behooveth you to return unto God even as ye were brought forth into existence, and to utter not such words as why or nay, if ye wish your creation to yield fruit at the time of your return. For none of you who have been born in the Bayán shall gain the fruit of your beginning unless ye return unto Him Whom God shall make manifest. He it is Who caused your beginning to proceed from God, and your return to be unto Him, did ye but know. *XVI, 15.*

How great the number of people who deck themselves with robes of silk all their lives, while clad in the garb of fire, inasmuch as they have divested themselves of the raiment of divine guidance and righteousness; and how numerous are those who wear clothes made of cotton or coarse wool throughout their lives, and yet by reason of their being endowed with the vesture of divine guidance and righteousness, are truly attired with the raiment of Paradise and take delight in the good-pleasure of God. Indeed it would be better in the sight of God were ye to combine the two, adorning yourselves with the raiment of divine guidance and righteousness and wearing exquisite silk, if ye can afford to do so. If not, at least act ye not unrighteously, but rather observe piety and virtue . . .

But for the sole reason of His being present amongst this people, We would have neither prescribed any law nor laid down any prohibition. It is only for the glorification of His Name and the exaltation of His Cause that We have enunciated certain laws at Our behest, or forbidden the acts to which We are averse, so that at the hour of His manifestation ye may attain through Him the good-pleasure of God and abstain from the things that are abhorrent unto Him.

Say, verily, the good-pleasure of Him Whom God shall make manifest is the good-pleasure of God, while the displeasure of Him Whom God shall make manifest is none other than the displeasure of God. Avoid ye His displeasure, and flee for refuge unto His good-pleasure. Say, the living guides to His good-pleasure are such as truly believe in Him and are well-assured in their faith, while the living testimonies of His displeasure are those who, when they hear the verses of God sent forth from His presence, or read the divine words revealed by Him, do not instantly embrace the Faith and attain unto certitude. *XVI, 14.*

6

EXCERPTS FROM
VARIOUS WRITINGS

A Y, God is the Lord and all are worshippers unto Him.

Say, God is the True One and all pay homage unto Him.

This is God, your Lord, and unto Him shall ye return.

Is there any doubt concerning God? He hath created you and all things. The Lord of all worlds is He.

S A Y, verily any one follower of this Faith can, by the leave of God, prevail over all who dwell in heaven and earth and in whatever lieth between them; for indeed this is, beyond the shadow of a doubt, the one true Faith. Therefore fear ye not, neither be ye grieved.

Say, God hath, according to that which is revealed in the Book, taken upon Himself the task of ensuring the ascendancy of any one of the followers of the Truth, over and above one hundred other souls, and the supremacy of one hundred believers over one thousand non-believers and the domination of one thousand of the faithful over all the peoples and kindreds of the earth; inasmuch as God calleth into being whatsoever He willeth by virtue of His behest. Verily He is potent over all things.

Say, the power of God is in the hearts of those who believe in the unity of God and bear witness that no God is there but Him, while the hearts of them that associate partners with God are impotent, devoid of life on this earth, for assuredly they are dead.

The Day is approaching when God will render the hosts

of Truth victorious, and He will purge the whole earth in such wise that within the compass of His knowledge not a single soul shall remain unless he truly believeth in God, worshippeth none other God but Him, boweth down by day and by night in His adoration, and is reckoned among such as are well assured.

Say, God indeed is the Sovereign Truth, Who is manifestly Supreme over His servants; He is the Help in Peril, the Self-Subsisting.

GOD testifieth that there is none other God but Him. His are the kingdoms in the heavens and on the earth and all that is between them. He is exalted above the comprehension of all things, and is inscrutable to the mind of every created being; none shall be able to fathom the oneness of His Being or to unravel the nature of His Existence. No peer or likeness, no similitude or equal can ever be joined with Him. Yield ye praise then unto Him and glorify Him and bear ye witness to the sanctity and oneness of His Being and magnify His might and majesty with wondrous glorification. This will enable you to gain admittance into the all-highest Paradise. Would that ye had firm faith in the revelation of the signs of God.

This is the divinely-inscribed Book. This is the outspread Tablet. Say, this indeed is the Frequented Fane, the sweet-scented Leaf, the Tree of divine Revelation, the surging Ocean, the Utterance which lay concealed, the Light above every light . . . Indeed every light is generated by God through the power of His behest. He of a truth is the Light in the kingdom of heaven and earth and whatever is between them. Through the radiance of His light God imparteth illumination to your hearts and maketh firm your steps, that perchance ye may yield praise unto Him.

Say, this of a certainty is the Garden of Repose, the loftiest Point of adoration, the Tree beyond which there is no passing, the blessed Lote-Tree, the Most Mighty Sign, the most beauteous Countenance and the most comely Face.

FROM the beginning that hath no beginning all men have bowed in adoration before Him Whom God shall make manifest and will continue to do so until the end that hath no end. How strange then that at the time of His appearance ye should pay homage by day and night unto that which the Point of the Bayán hath enjoined upon you and yet fail to worship Him Whom God shall make manifest.

CONSECRATE Thou, O my God, the whole of this Tree unto Him, that from it may be revealed all the fruits created by God within it for Him through Whom God hath willed to reveal all that He pleaseth. By Thy glory! I have not wished that this Tree should ever bear any branch, leaf, or fruit that would fail to bow down before Him, on the day of His Revelation, or refuse to laud Thee through Him, as beseemeth the glory of His all-glorious Revelation, and the sublimity of His most sublime Concealment. And shouldst Thou behold, O my God, any branch, leaf, or fruit upon Me that hath failed to bow down before

Him, on the day of His Revelation, cut it off, O My God, from that Tree, for it is not of Me, nor shall it return unto Me.

H E—glorified be His mention—resembleth the sun. Were unnumbered mirrors to be placed before it, each would, according to its capacity, reflect the splendour of that sun, and were none to be placed before it, it would still continue to rise and set, and the mirrors alone would be veiled from its light. I, verily, have not fallen short of My duty to admonish that people, and to devise means whereby they may turn towards God, their Lord, and believe in God, their Creator. If, on the day of His Revelation, all that are on earth bear Him allegiance, Mine inmost being will rejoice, inasmuch as all will have attained the summit of their existence, and will have been brought face to face with their Beloved, and will have recognized, to the fullest extent attainable in the world of being, the splendour of Him Who is the Desire of their hearts. If not, My soul will indeed be saddened. I truly have nurtured all things for this purpose. How, then, can anyone be veiled from Him? For this have I called upon God, and will continue to call upon Him. He, verily, is nigh, ready to answer.

T H E glory of Him Whom God shall make manifest is immeasurably above every other glory, and His majesty is far above every other majesty. His beauty excelleth every other embodiment of beauty, and His grandeur immensely exceedeth every other manifestation of grandeur. Every light paleth before the radiance of His light, and every other exponent of mercy falleth short before the tokens of His mercy. Every other perfection is as naught in face of His consummate perfection, and every other display of might is as nothing before His absolute might. His names are superior to all other names. His good-pleasure taketh precedence over any other expression of good-pleasure. His pre-eminent exaltation is far above the reach of every other symbol of exaltation. The splendour of His appearance far surpasseth that of any other appearance. His divine concealment is far more profound than any other concealment. His loftiness is immeasurably above every other loftiness. His gracious favour is unequalled by any other evidence of favour. His power transcendeth every power. His sovereignty is invincible in the face of every other sovereignty. His celestial dominion is exalted far above every other dominion. His knowledge pervadeth all created things, and His consummate power extendeth over all beings.

ALL men have proceeded from God and unto Him shall all return. All shall appear before Him for judgement. He is the Lord of the Day of Resurrection, of Regeneration and of Reckoning, and His revealed Word is the Balance.

True death is realized when a person dieth to himself at the time of His Revelation in such wise that he seeketh naught except Him.

True resurrection from the sepulchres means to be quickened in conformity with His Will, through the power of His utterance.

Paradise is attainment of His good-pleasure and everlasting hell-fire His judgement through justice.

The Day He revealeth Himself is Resurrection Day which shall last as long as He ordaineth.

Everything belongeth unto Him and is fashioned by Him. All besides Him are His creatures.

In the Name of God, the Most Exalted, the Most High.

VERILY I am God, no God is there but Me, and aught except Me is but My creation. Say, worship Me then, O ye, My creatures.

I have called Thee into being, have nurtured Thee, protected Thee, loved Thee, raised Thee up and have graciously chosen Thee to be the manifestation of Mine Own Self, that Thou mayest recite My verses as ordained by Me, and may summon whomsoever I have created unto My Religion which is none other than this glorious and exalted Path.

I have fashioned all created things for Thy sake, and I have, by virtue of My Will, set Thee sovereign Ruler over all mankind. Moreover, I have decreed that whoso embraceth My religion shall believe in My unity, and I have linked this belief with remembrance of Thee, and after

Thee the remembrance of such as Thou hast, by My leave, caused to be the 'Letters of the Living', and of whatever hath been revealed from My religion in the Bayán. This, indeed, is what will enable the sincere among My servants to gain admittance into the celestial Paradise.

Verily, the sun is but a token from My presence so that the true believers among My servants may discern in its rising the dawning of every Dispensation.

In truth I have created Thee through Thyself, then at My Own behest I have fashioned all things through the creative power of Thy Word. We are All-Powerful. I have appointed Thee to be the Beginning and the End, the Seen and the Hidden. Verily We are the All-Knowing.

No one hath been or will ever be invested with prophethood other than Thee, nor hath any sacred Book been or will be revealed unto any one except Thee. Such is the decree ordained by Him Who is the All-Encompassing, the Best Beloved.

The Bayán is in truth Our conclusive proof for all created things, and all the peoples of the world are powerless before the revelation of its verses. It enshrineth the sum total of all the Scriptures, whether of the past or of the future, even as Thou art the Repository of all Our proofs in this Day. We cause whomsoever We desire to be admitted into the gardens of our most holy, most sublime Paradise. Thus is divine revelation inaugurated in each Dispensation at Our behest. We are truly the supreme Ruler. Indeed no religion shall We ever inaugurate unless it be renewed in the days to come. This is a promise We solemnly have made. Verily We are supreme over all things . . .

He is God, the Sovereign Lord, the All-Glorious.

S AY: Praise be to God Who graciously enableth whomsoever He willeth to adore Him. Verily no God is there but Him. His are the most excellent titles; it is He Who causeth His Word to be fulfilled as He pleaseth and it is He Who leadeth those who have received illumination and seek the way of righteousness.

Fear thou God, thy Lord, and make mention of His Name in the day-time and at eventide. Follow not the promptings of the faithless, lest thou be reckoned among the exponents of idle fancies. Faithfully obey the Primal Point Who is the Lord Himself, and be of the righteous. Let nothing cause thee to be sore shaken, neither let the things which have been destined to take place in this Cause disturb thee. Strive earnestly for the sake of God and walk in the path of righteousness. Shouldst thou encounter the unbelievers, place thy whole trust in God, thy Lord, saying, Sufficient is God unto me in the kingdoms of both this world and the next.

The Day is approaching when God shall bring the faithful together. In truth no God is there other than Him.

May the peace of God be with those who have been guided aright through the power of divine guidance.

He is God, the Supreme Ruler, the Sovereign Truth,
He Whose help is implored by all.

G LORIFIED is He to Whom pertaineth the dominion of the heavens and of the earth, in Whose hand lieth the kingdom of all created things and unto Whom shall all return. It is He Who setteth the measure assigned to each and every thing and revealeth His goodly gifts and blessings in His sacred Book for the benefit of those who offer gratitude for His Cause.

Say, this earthly life shall come to an end, and everyone shall expire and return unto my Lord God Who will reward with the choicest gifts the deeds of those who endure with patience. Verily thy God assigneth the measure of all created things as He willeth, by virtue of His behest; and those who conform to the good-pleasure of your Lord, they are indeed among the blissful.

Thy Lord hath never raised up a prophet in the past who failed to summon the people to His Lord, and today is truly similar to the times of old, were ye to ponder over the verses revealed by God.

When God sent forth His Prophet Muḥammad, on that day the termination of the prophetic cycle was foreordained in the knowledge of God. Yea, that promise hath indeed come true and the decree of God hath been accomplished as He hath ordained. Assuredly we are today living in the Days of God. These are the glorious days on the like of which the sun hath never risen in the past. These are the days which the people in bygone times eagerly expected. What hath then befallen you that ye are fast asleep? These are the days wherein God hath caused the Day-Star of Truth to shine resplendent. What hath then caused you to keep your silence? These are the appointed days which ye have been yearningly awaiting in the past—the days of the advent of divine justice. Render ye thanks unto God, O ye concourse of believers.

Let not the deeds of those who reject the Truth shut you out as by a veil. Such people have warrant over your bodies only, and God hath not reposed in them power over your spirits, your souls and your hearts. Fear ye God that haply it may be well with you. All things have been created for your sakes, and for the sake of naught else hath your creation been ordained. Fear ye God and take heed lest forms and apparels debar you from recognizing Him. Render ye thanksgiving unto God that perchance He may deal mercifully with you.

This mortal life is sure to perish; its pleasures are bound to fade away and ere long ye shall return unto God, distressed with pangs of remorse, for presently ye shall be roused from your slumber, and ye shall soon find yourselves in the presence of God and will be asked of your doings.

Say, how dare ye flagrantly deny the verses sent down from the heaven of justice, yet ye read the Books of God revealed in the past? How do ye repudiate the meeting with your Lord which was appointed with you aforetime, and fail in this Day to heed His warning? Indeed, by adhering to forms and by following the promptings of your selfish desires, ye have deprived yourselves of the good-pleasure of your Lord, except those whom their Lord hath endowed with knowledge and who in this Day render thanks unto Him for the bounty of being identified with the true Faith of God. Therefore announce ye the Message unto those who manifest virtue and teach them the ways of the One True God, that haply they may comprehend.

Withhold thy tongue from uttering that which might grieve thee and beseech God for mercy. Verily He is fully cognizant of the righteous, for He is with such of His servants as truly believe in Him, and He is not unaware of the actions of the mischief-makers, inasmuch as nothing whatever in the heavens or on the earth can escape His knowledge.

These verses, clear and conclusive, are a token of the mercy of thy Lord and a source of guidance for all mankind. They are a light unto those who believe in them and a fire of afflictive torment for those who turn away and reject them.

O THOU who art the chosen one among women!

He is God; glorified is the splendour of His light.

The verses in this Tablet are revealed for the one who hath believed in the signs of her Lord and is reckoned among such as are wholly devoted unto Him. Bear thou witness that verily no God is there but Him, Who is both my Lord and thine, and that no other God besides Him existeth. He is the Bountiful, the Almighty.

Yield thee thanks unto God, for He hath graciously aided thee in this Day, revealed for thee the clear verses of this Tablet, and hath numbered thee among such women as have believed in the signs of God, have taken Him as their guardian and are of the grateful. Verily God shall soon reward thee and those who have believed in His signs with an excellent reward from His presence. Assuredly no God is there other than Him, the All-Possessing, the Most Generous. The revelations of His bounty pervade all created things; He is the Merciful, the Compassionate.

GOD testifieth that there is none other God but Him, the Almighty, the Best Beloved.

Fix your gaze upon Him Whom God shall make manifest in the Day of Resurrection, then firmly believe in that which is sent down by Him.

Say, God hath undisputed triumph over every victorious one. There is no one in heaven or earth or in whatever lieth between them who can frustrate the transcendent supremacy of His triumph. He calleth into being whatsoever He willeth through the potency of His behest. Verily God is the mightiest Sustainer, the Helper and the Defender.

WHEN the Day-Star of Bahá will shine resplendent above the horizon of eternity it is incumbent upon you to present yourselves before His Throne. Beware lest ye be seated in His presence or ask questions without His leave. Fear ye God, O concourse of the Mirrors.

Beg ye of Him the wondrous tokens of His favour that He may graciously reveal for you whatever He willeth and desireth, inasmuch as on that Day all the revelations of divine bounty shall circle around the Seat of His glory and emanate from His presence, could ye but understand it.

It behooveth you to remain silent before His Throne, for indeed of all the things which have been created between heaven and earth nothing on that Day will be deemed more fitting than the observance of silence. Moreover, take ye good heed not to be reckoned among those of the past who were invested with knowledge, yet by reason of their learning waxed proud before God, the Transcendent, the Self-Subsisting, inasmuch as on that Day it is He Who is the All-Knowing, the Omniscient, the Source of all knowledge, far above such as are endued with learning; and it is

He Who is the Potent, the All-Compelling, the Lord of power, in the face of those who wield power; and it is He Who is the Mighty, the Most August, the Most Glorious before such as display glory; and on that Day it is He Who is the Lofty, the All-Highest, the Source of exaltation, far above those who are elevated in rank; and it is He Who is the Almighty, the Source of glory and grandeur, far above the pomp of the mighty; and it is He Who is the Omnipotent, the Supreme Ruler, the Lord of judgement, transcending all such as are invested with authority; and it is He Who is the Generous, the Most Benevolent, the Essence of bounty, Who standeth supreme in the face of such as show benevolence; and it is He Who is the Ordainer and the Supreme Wielder of authority and power, inconceivably high above those who hold earthly dominion; and it is He Who is the Most Excellent, the Unsurpassed, the Pre-eminent in the face of every man of accomplishment.

Ye have, one and all, been called into being to seek His presence and to attain that exalted and glorious station. Indeed, He will send down from the heaven of His mercy that which will benefit you, and whatever is graciously vouchsafed by Him shall enable you to dispense with all mankind. Verily on that Day the learning of the learned shall prove of no avail, neither the accomplishments of the exponents of knowledge, nor the pomp of the highly honoured, nor the power of the mighty, nor the remembrance of the devout, nor the deeds of the righteous, nor the genuflexion of the kneeling worshipper, nor his prostration or turning towards the Qiblih, nor the honour of the honoured, nor the kinship of the highly born, nor the nobility of those of noble descent, nor the discourse of the eloquent, nor the titles of the prominent—none of these shall be of any avail unto them—inasmuch as all these and whatever else ye have known or comprehended were created by His word of command 'Be' and it is. Indeed if it be His Will He can assuredly bring about the resurrection of all created things through a word from Himself. He is, in truth, over and above all this, the All-Powerful, the Almighty, the Omnipotent.

Beware, O concourse of Mirrors, lest on that Day titles make you vainglorious. Know ye of a certainty that ye, together with all those who stand above you or below you, have been created for that Day. Fear ye God and commit not that which would grieve His heart, nor be of them that have gone astray. Perchance He will appear invested with the power of Truth while ye are fast asleep on your couches, or His messengers will bring glorious and resplendent Tablets from Him while ye turn away disdainfully from Him, pronounce sentence against Him—such sentence as ye would never pass on yourselves—and say, 'This is not from God, the All-Subduing, the Self-Existent'.

Glory be unto Thee, O my God, Thou art well aware that I have proclaimed Thy Word and have not failed in the mission Thou didst enjoin upon me. I entreat Thee to guard the people of the Bayán on that Day in order that they may not pronounce censure against Thee nor contend with Thy signs. Protect them then, O my God, through the power of Thy might which pervadeth all mankind.

He is the Almighty.

GLORY be unto Him Who is the Lord of all that are in the heavens and on the earth; He is the All-Wise, the All-

Informed. It is He Who calleth into being whatsoever He willeth at His behest; He is indeed the Clement, the Fashioner. Say, verily He is equal to His purpose; whomsoever He willeth, He maketh victorious through the power of His hosts; there is none other God but Him, the Mighty, the Wise. His is the kingdom of earth and heaven and He is the Lord of power and glory. Such as have believed in God and in His signs are indeed the followers of truth and shall abide in the gardens of delight, while those who have disbelieved in God and have rejected that which He hath revealed, these shall be the inmates of the fire wherein they shall remain forever. Say, most people have openly repudiated God and have followed the rebellious wicked doers. Such people resemble those who have gone before them, upholding every hostile oppressor. Verily no God is there but God; His is the kingdom of heaven and earth and He is the Clement, the All-Knowing. God testifieth that there is no God but Him, and He Who speaketh at the bidding of His Lord is but the First to worship Him. He is the peerless Creator Who hath created the heavens and the earth and whatsoever lieth between them, and all do His bidding. He is the One Whose grace hath encompassed all that are in the heavens, on earth or elsewhere, and everyone abideth by His behest.

IT behooveth you to await the Day of the appearance of Him Whom God shall manifest. Indeed My aim in planting the Tree of the Bayán hath been none other than to enable you to recognize Me. In truth I Myself am the first to bow down before God and to believe in Him. Therefore let not your recognition become fruitless, inasmuch as the Bayán, notwithstanding the sublimity of its station, beareth fealty to Him Whom God shall make manifest, and it is He Who beseemeth most to be acclaimed as the Seat of divine Reality, though indeed He is I and I am He. However, when the Tree of the Bayán attaineth its highest development, We shall bend it low as a token of adoration towards its Lord Who will appear in the person of Him Whom God shall make manifest. Perchance ye may be privileged to glorify God as it befitteth His august Self.

Indeed ye have been called into being through the power of the Point of the Bayán while the Point Himself is resigned to the Will of Him Whom God shall make manifest, is exalted through His transcendent sublimity, is sustained by the evidences of His might, is glorified by the majesty of His oneness, is adorned by the beauty of His singleness, is empowered by His eternal dominion and is invested with authority through His everlasting sovereignty. How then could they, who are but the creation of the Point, be justified in saying 'why or wherefore'?

O congregation of the Bayán, and all who are therein! Recognize ye the limits imposed upon you, for such a One as the Point of the Bayán Himself hath believed in Him Whom God shall make manifest, before all things were created. Therein, verily, do I glory before all who are in the kingdom of heaven and earth. Suffer not yourselves to be shut out as by a veil from God after He hath revealed Himself. For all that hath been exalted in the Bayán is but as a ring upon My hand, and I Myself am, verily, but a ring upon the hand of Him Whom God shall make manifest— glorified be His mention! He turneth it as He pleaseth, for whatsoever He pleaseth, and through whatsoever He pleaseth. He, verily, is the Help in Peril, the Most High.

7

PRAYERS AND MEDITATIONS

In the Name of God, the Lord of overpowering majesty,
the All-Compelling.

ALLOWED be the Lord in Whose hand is the source of dominion. He createth whatsoever He willeth by His Word of command 'Be', and it is. His hath been the power of authority heretofore and it shall remain His hereafter. He maketh victorious whomsoever He pleaseth, through the potency of His behest. He is in truth the Powerful, the Almighty. Unto Him pertaineth all glory and majesty in the kingdoms of Revelation and Creation and whatever lieth between them. Verily He is the Potent, the All-Glorious. From everlasting He hath been the Source of indomitable strength and shall remain so unto everlasting. He is indeed the Lord of might and power. All the kingdoms of heaven and earth and whatever is between them are God's, and His power is supreme over all things. All the treasures of earth and heaven and everything between them are His, and His protection extendeth over all things. He is the Creator of the heavens and the earth and whatever lieth between them and He truly is a witness over all things. He is the Lord of Reckoning for all that dwell in the heavens and on earth and whatever lieth between them, and truly God is swift to reckon. He setteth the measure assigned to all who are in the heavens and the earth and whatever is between them. Verily He is the Supreme Protector. He holdeth in His grasp the keys of heaven and earth and of everything between them. At His Own pleasure doth He bestow gifts, through the power of His command. Indeed His grace encompasseth all and He is the All-Knowing.

Say: God sufficeth unto me; He is the One Who holdeth in His grasp the kingdom of all things. Through the power of His hosts of heaven and earth and whatever lieth between them, He protecteth whomsoever among His servants He willeth. God, in truth, keepeth watch over all things.

Immeasurably exalted art Thou, O Lord! Protect us from what lieth in front of us and behind us, above our heads, on our right, on our left, below our feet and every other side to which we are exposed. Verily Thy protection over all things is unfailing.[1]

SEND down Thy blessings, O my God, upon the Tree of the Bayán, upon its root and its branch, its boughs, its leaves, its fruits and upon whatsoever it beareth or sheltereth. Cause this Tree then to be made into a magnificent Scroll to be offered to the presence of Him Whom Thou wilt make manifest on the Day of Judgement, that He may graciously allow the entire company of the followers of the Bayán to be restored to life and that He may, through His bounty, inaugurate a new creation.

Indeed all are but paupers in the face of Thy tender mercy, and lowly servants before the tokens of Thy loving-kindness. I beg of Thee, by Thy bounty, O my God, and by the outpourings of Thy mercy and bestowals, O my Lord, and by the evidences of Thy heavenly favours and grace, O my Best Beloved, to watch over Him Whom God shall make manifest that no trace of despondency may ever touch Him.

[1] The original of this prayer for protection is written in the Báb's own hand, in the form of a pentacle.

Immeasurably glorified and exalted art Thou. How can I make mention of Thee, O Thou the Beloved of the entire creation; and how can I acknowledge Thy claim, O Thou, before Whom every created thing standeth in awe. The loftiest station to which human perception can soar and the utmost height which the minds and souls of men can scale are but signs created through the potency of Thy command and tokens manifested through the power of Thy Revelation. Far be it from Thy glory that anyone other than Thee should make mention of Thee or should attempt to voice Thy praise. The very essence of every reality beareth witness to its debarment from the precincts of the court of Thy nearness, and the quintessence of every being testifieth to its failure to attain Thy holy Presence. Immeasurably glorified and exalted art Thou! That which alone beseemeth Thee is the befitting mention made by Thine Own Self, and that only which is worthy of Thee is the anthem of praise voiced by Thine Own Essence . . .

Through the revelation of Thy grace, O Lord, Thou didst call Me into being on a night such as this,[1] and lo, I am now lonely and forsaken in a mountain. Praise and thanksgiving be unto Thee for whatever conformeth to Thy pleasure within the empire of heaven and earth. And all sovereignty is Thine, extending beyond the uttermost range of the kingdoms of Revelation and Creation.

Thou didst create Me, O Lord, through Thy gracious favour and didst protect Me through Thy bounty in the darkness of the womb and didst nourish Me, through Thy loving-kindness, with life-giving blood. After having fashioned Me in a most comely form, through Thy tender providence, and having perfected My creation through

[1] Refers to the Báb's birthday on the first day of the month of Muḥarram, 1235 A.H. (October 20, 1819).

Thine excellent handiwork and breathed Thy Spirit into My body through Thine infinite mercy and by the revelation of Thy transcendent unity, Thou didst cause Me to issue forth from the world of concealment into the visible world, naked, ignorant of all things, and powerless to achieve aught. Thou didst then nourish Me with refreshing milk and didst rear Me in the arms of My parents with manifest compassion, until Thou didst graciously acquaint Me with the realities of Thy Revelation and apprised Me of the straight path of Thy Faith as set forth in Thy Book. And when I attained full maturity Thou didst cause Me to bear allegiance unto Thine inaccessible Remembrance, and enabled Me to advance towards the designated station, where Thou didst educate Me through the subtle operations of Thy handiwork and didst nurture Me in that land with Thy most gracious gifts. When that which had been preordained in Thy Book came to pass Thou didst cause Me, through Thy kindness, to reach Thy holy precincts and didst suffer Me, through Thy tender mercy, to dwell within the court of fellowship, until I discerned therein that which I discerned of the clear tokens of Thy mercifulness, the compelling evidences of Thy oneness, the effulgent splendours of Thy majesty, the source of Thy supreme singleness, the heights of Thy transcendent sovereignty, the signs of Thy peerlessness, the manifestations of Thine exalted glory, the retreats of Thy sanctity, and whatsoever is inscrutable to all but Thee.

VERILY I am Thy servant, O my God, and Thy poor one and Thy suppliant and Thy wretched creature. I have arrived at Thy gate, seeking Thy shelter. I have found no contentment save in Thy love, no exultation except in Thy remembrance, no eagerness but in obedience to Thee, no joy save in Thy nearness, and no tranquillity except in reunion with Thee, notwithstanding that I am conscious that all created things are debarred from Thy sublime Essence and the entire creation is denied access to Thine inmost Being. Whenever I attempt to approach Thee, I perceive nothing in myself but the tokens of Thy grace and behold naught in my being but the revelations of Thy loving-kindness. How can one who is but Thy creature seek reunion with Thee and attain unto Thy presence, whereas no created thing can ever be associated with Thee, nor can aught comprehend Thee? How is it possible for a lowly servant to recognize Thee and to extol Thy praise, notwithstanding that Thou hast destined for him the revelations of Thy dominion and the wondrous testimonies of Thy sovereignty? Thus every created thing beareth witness that it is debarred from the sanctuary of Thy presence by reason of the limitations imposed upon its inner reality. It is undisputed, however, that the influence of Thine attraction hath everlastingly been inherent in the realities of Thy handiwork, although that which beseemeth the hallowed court of Thy providence is exalted beyond the attainment of the entire creation. This indicateth, O my God, my utter powerlessness to praise Thee and revealeth my utmost impotence in yielding thanks unto Thee; and how much more to attain the recognition of Thy divine unity or to succeed in reaching the clear tokens of Thy praise, Thy sanctity and Thy glory. Nay, by Thy might, I yearn for naught but Thine Own Self and seek no one other than Thee.

MAGNIFIED be Thy Name, O God. Thine in truth are the Kingdoms of Creation and Revelation, and verily in our Lord have we placed our whole trust. All praise be unto Thee, O God; Thou art the Maker of the heavens and the earth and that which is between them, and Thou in truth art the supreme Ruler, the Fashioner, the All-Wise. Glorified art Thou, O Lord! Thou wilt surely gather mankind for the Day of whose coming there is no doubt—the Day whereon everyone shall appear before Thee and find life in Thee. This is the Day of the One true God—the Day Thou shalt bring about as Thou pleasest through the power of Thy behest.

Thou art the Sovereign, the wondrous Creator, the Mighty, the Best Beloved.

LAUDED be Thy Name, O God. Thou art in truth our Lord; Thou art aware of whatsoever is in the heavens and on the earth. Send down then upon us a token of Thy mercy. Verily Thou art unsurpassed among them that show mercy. All praise be unto Thee, O Lord. Ordain for us from Thy presence that which will comfort the hearts of the sincere among Thy servants. Glorified art Thou, O God, Thou art the Creator of the heavens and the earth and that which lieth between them. Thou art the sovereign Lord, the Most Holy, the Almighty, the All-Wise. Magnified be Thy Name, O God, send down upon them who have believed in God and in His signs a mighty succour from Thy presence such as to enable them to prevail over the generality of mankind.

GLORY be unto Thee, O God. How can I make mention of Thee while Thou art sanctified from the praise of all mankind. Magnified be Thy Name, O God, Thou art the King, the Eternal Truth; Thou knowest what is in the heavens and on the earth, and unto Thee must all return. Thou hast sent down Thy divinely-ordained Revelation according to a clear measure. Praised art Thou, O Lord! At Thy behest Thou dost render victorious whomsoever Thou willest, through the hosts of heaven and earth and whatsoever existeth between them. Thou art the Sovereign, the Eternal Truth, the Lord of invincible might.

Glorified art Thou, O Lord, Thou forgivest at all times the sins of such among Thy servants as implore Thy pardon. Wash away my sins and the sins of those who seek Thy forgiveness at dawn, who pray to Thee in the day-time and in the night season, who yearn after naught save God, who offer up whatsoever God hath graciously bestowed upon them, who celebrate Thy praise at morn and eventide, and who are not remiss in their duties.

PRAISE be unto Thee, O Lord. Forgive us our sins, have mercy upon us and enable us to return unto Thee. Suffer us not to rely on aught else besides Thee, and vouchsafe unto us, through Thy bounty, that which Thou lovest and desirest and well beseemeth Thee. Exalt the station of them that have truly believed and forgive them with Thy gracious forgiveness. Verily Thou art the Help in Peril, the Self-Subsisting.

O GOD our Lord! Protect us through Thy grace from whatsoever may be repugnant unto Thee and vouchsafe unto us that which well beseemeth Thee. Give us more out of Thy bounty and bless us. Pardon us for the things we have done and wash away our sins and forgive us with Thy gracious forgiveness. Verily Thou art the Most Exalted, the Self-Subsisting.

Thy loving providence hath encompassed all created things in the heavens and on the earth, and Thy forgiveness hath surpassed the whole creation. Thine is sovereignty; in Thy hand are the Kingdoms of Creation and Revelation; in Thy right hand Thou holdest all created things and within Thy grasp are the assigned measures of forgiveness. Thou forgivest whomsoever among Thy servants Thou pleasest. Verily Thou art the Ever-Forgiving, the All-Loving. Nothing whatsoever escapeth Thy knowledge, and naught is there which is hidden from Thee.

O God our Lord! Protect us through the potency of Thy might, enable us to enter Thy wondrous surging ocean, and grant us that which well befitteth Thee.

Thou art the Sovereign Ruler, the Mighty Doer, the Exalted, the All-loving.

GLORY be unto Thee, O Lord my God! Nothing whatsoever escapeth Thy knowledge, nor is there anything that could slip from Thy grasp, or anything that could thwart Thy Purpose, whether in the heavens or on the earth, of the past or of the future.

Thou seest Paradise and the inmates thereof; Thou beholdest the realm below and the dwellers thereof. All are but Thy servants and are held within Thy grasp.

O Lord! Render victorious Thy forbearing servants in Thy days by granting them a befitting victory, inasmuch as they have sought martyrdom in Thy path. Send down upon them that which will bring comfort to their minds, will rejoice their inner beings, will impart assurance to their hearts and tranquillity to their bodies and will enable their souls to ascend to the presence of God, the Most Exalted, and to attain the supreme Paradise and such retreats of glory as Thou hast destined for men of true knowledge and virtue. Verily Thou knowest all things, while we are but Thy servants, Thy thralls, Thy bondsmen and Thy poor ones. No Lord but Thee do we invoke, O God our Lord, nor do we implore blessings or grace from anyone but Thee, O Thou Who art the God of mercy unto this world and the next. We are but the embodiments of poverty, of nothingness, of helplessness and of perdition, while Thy whole Being betokeneth wealth, independence, glory, majesty and boundless grace.

Turn our recompense, O Lord, into that which well beseemeth Thee of the good of this world and of the next, and of the manifold bounties which extend from on high down to the earth below.

Verily Thou art our Lord and the Lord of all things. Into Thy hands do we surrender ourselves, yearning for the things that pertain unto Thee.

GLORIFIED be Thy Name, O Lord! In whom shall I take refuge while Thou art in truth my God and my Beloved; unto whom shall I turn for shelter while Thou art my Lord and my Possessor; and towards whom shall I flee while Thou art in truth my Master and my Sanctuary; and whom shall I implore while Thou art in truth my Treasure and the Goal of my desire; and through whom shall I plead before Thee, while Thou art in truth my highest aspiration and supreme desire? Every hope hath been frustrated save the yearning for Thy heavenly grace, and every door is barred except the portal leading to the well-spring of Thy blessings.

I beseech Thee, O my Lord, by Thy most effulgent splendour, before whose brightness every soul humbly boweth down and prostrateth itself in adoration for Thy sake—a splendour before whose radiance fire is turned into light, the dead are brought to life and every difficulty is changed into ease. I entreat Thee by this great, this wondrous splendour and by the glory of Thine exalted sovereignty, O Thou Who art the Lord of indomitable power, to transform us through Thy bounty into that which Thou Thyself dost possess and enable us to become fountains of Thy light, and graciously vouchsafe unto us that which beseemeth the majesty of Thy transcendent dominion. For unto Thee have I raised my hands, O Lord, and in Thee have I found sheltering support, O Lord, and unto Thee have I resigned myself, O Lord, and upon Thee have I placed my whole reliance, O Lord, and by Thee am I strengthened, O Lord.

Verily there is no power nor strength except in Thee.

THOU art aware, O My God, that since the day Thou didst call Me into being out of the water of Thy love till I reached fifteen years of age I lived in the land which witnessed My birth [Shíráz]. Then Thou didst enable Me to go to the seaport [Búshihr] where for five years I was engaged in trading with the goodly gifts of Thy realm and was occupied in that with which Thou hast favoured Me through the wondrous essence of Thy loving-kindness. I procceded therefrom to the Holy Land [Karbilá] where I sojourned for one year. Then I returned to the place of My birth. There I experienced the revelation of Thy sublime bestowals and the evidences of Thy boundless grace. I yield Thee praise for all Thy goodly gifts and I render Thee thanksgiving for all Thy bounties. Then at the age of twenty-five I proceeded to thy sacred House [Mecca], and by the time I returned to the place where I was born, a year had elapsed. There I tarried patiently in the path of Thy love and beheld the evidences of Thy manifold bounties and of Thy loving-kindness until Thou didst ordain for Me to set out in Thy direction and to migrate to Thy presence. Thus I departed therefrom by Thy leave, spending six months in the land of Şád [Iṣfáhán] and seven months in the First Mountain [Mákú], where Thou didst rain down upon Me that which beseemeth the glory of Thy heavenly blessings and befitteth the sublimity of Thy gracious gifts and favours. Now, in My thirtieth year, Thou beholdest Me, O My God, in this Grievous Mountain [Chihríq] where I have dwelt for one whole year.

Praise be unto Thee, O My Lord, for all times, heretofore and hereafter; and thanks be unto Thee, O My God, under all conditions, whether of the past or the future. The gifts Thou hast bestowed upon Me have reached their fullest measure and the blessings Thou hast vouchsafed unto Me have attained their consummation. Naught do I now witness but the manifold evidences of Thy grace and loving-kindness, Thy bounty and gracious favours, Thy generosity and loftiness, Thy sovereignty and might, Thy splendour and Thy glory, and that which befitteth the holy court of Thy transcendent dominion and majesty and beseemeth the glorious precincts of Thine eternity and exaltation.

I AM aware, O Lord, that my trespasses have covered my face with shame in Thy presence, and have burdened my back before Thee, have intervened between me and Thy beauteous countenance, have compassed me from every direction and have hindered me on all sides from gaining access unto the revelations of Thy celestial power.

O Lord! If Thou forgivest me not, who is there then to grant pardon, and if Thou hast no mercy upon me who is capable of showing compassion? Glory be unto Thee, Thou didst create me when I was non-existent and Thou didst nourish me while I was devoid of any understanding. Praise be unto Thee, every evidence of bounty proceedeth from Thee and every token of grace emanateth from the treasuries of Thy decree.

I BEG Thee to forgive me, O my Lord, for every mention but the mention of Thee, and for every praise but the praise of Thee, and for every delight but delight in Thy nearness, and for every pleasure but the pleasure of communion with Thee, and for every joy but the joy of Thy love and of Thy good-pleasure, and for all things pertaining

unto me which bear no relationship unto Thee, O Thou
Who art the Lord of lords, He Who provideth the means
and unlocketh the doors.

How can I praise Thee, O Lord, for the evidences of Thy
mighty splendour and for Thy wondrous sweet savours
which Thou hast imparted to Me in this fortress, in such
measure that nothing in the heavens or on the earth can
compare with them? Thou hast watched over Me in the
heart of this mountain where I am compassed by mountains
on all sides. One hangeth above Me, others stand on My
right and My left and yet another riseth in front of Me.
Glory be unto Thee, no God is there but Thee. How often
have I seen rocks from the mountain hurtling down upon
Me, and Thou didst protect Me therefrom and preserved
Me within the stronghold of Thy divine Unity.

Glorified and exalted art Thou, and praise be unto Thee
for whatsoever Thou lovest and desirest, and thanks be
unto Thee for that which Thou hast decreed and pre-
ordained. From time immemorial Thy tender mercy hath
been sent down and the process of Thy creation hath been
and ever is ceaseless. Thy handiwork is unlike the work of
anyone besides Thee, and Thy goodly gifts are unparalleled
by the gifts of anyone other than Thyself.

Praise be unto Thee, O My Beloved, and magnified be
Thy Name. Ever since the hour I set foot upon this fortress till the moment I shall have departed therefrom, I
behold Thee established upon Thy seat of glory and
majesty, sending down upon Me the manifold tokens of
Thy bountiful favour and grace. Thou beholdest that My

dwelling place is but the heart of the mountains, and Thou discernest naught in My Person except the evidences of abasement and loneliness.

Lauded be Thy Name; I render Thee thanks for every instance of Thine inscrutable Decree and offer My praise for every token of Thy tribulations. Having suffered Me to be cast into the prison, Thou didst turn it into a garden of Paradise for Me and caused it to become a chamber of the court of everlasting fellowship.

How numerous the verses Thou didst send down unto Me, and the prayers Thou didst hear Me offer unto Thee. How diverse the revelations which Thou didst call into being through Me and the experiences Thou didst witness in Me.

Magnified be Thy Name. Manifold trials have been powerless to deter Me from yielding thanks unto Thee and My shortcomings have failed to keep Me back from extolling Thy virtues. The infidels had purposed to turn My abode into one of disgrace and humiliation. But Thou hast glorified Me through My remembrance of Thee, hast exalted Me through My praise of Thee, hast graciously aided Me through the revelations of Thy oneness, and hast conferred upon Me a great honour through the effulgent splendours of Thine ancient eternity. To the fire Thou dost command, 'Be thou a soothing balm unto My Servant', and to the prison, 'Be thou a seat of tender compassion to My Servant, as a token from My presence'. Yea, I swear by Thy glory; to Me the prison hath proved to be naught but the most delightful garden of Paradise and hath served as the noblest spot in the realm above.

Praised and glorified art Thou. How often did adversities descend upon Me and Thou didst temper them and avert them through Thy gracious favour; and how many

times were commotions stirred up against Me at the hand
of the people, while Thou didst cause them to subside
through Thy tender mercy. How numerous the occasions
when the Nimrods kindled fires wherewith to burn Me,
but Thou didst make them balm for Me; and how manifold the instances when the infidels decreed My humiliation and Thou didst turn them into marks of honour for
Me...

Verily Thou art the highest aspiration of every earnest
seeker and the Goal of the desire of them that yearn after
Thee. Thou art He Who is ready to answer the call of such
as recognize Thy divine unity, and He before Whom the
faint-hearted stand in awe. Thou art the Helper of the
needy, the Deliverer of the captives, the Abaser of the
oppressors, the Destroyer of the wrong-doers, the God of
all men, the Lord of all created things. Thine are the kingdoms of Creation and Revelation, O Thou Who art the
Lord of all the worlds.

O All-Sufficient One! Thou dost suffice Me in every
hardship that may descend upon Me and in every affliction
that may wax great before Me. Thou art My sole Com-
panion in My loneliness, the Delight of My heart in My
solitude and My Best Beloved in My prison and in My
Abode. No God is there but Thee!

Whomsoever Thou dost suffice shall not be put to grief;
whomsoever Thou dost protect shall never perish; whomsoever Thou dost help shall never be abased; and he unto
whom Thou turnest Thy gaze shall never be far removed
from Thee.

Write down for us then whatsoever is of Thee, and forgive us for what we are. Verily Thou art the Lord of power
and glory, the Lord of all the worlds. 'Far be the glory of
Thy Lord, the Lord of all greatness, from what they impute

to Him, and peace be upon His Apostles, and praise be unto God, the Lord of all the worlds.'[1]

GLORY be to Thee, O God! Thou art the God Who hath existed before all things, Who will exist after all things and will last beyond all things. Thou art the God Who knoweth all things, and is supreme over all things. Thou art the God Who dealeth mercifully with all things, Who judgeth between all things and Whose vision embraceth all things. Thou art God my Lord, Thou art aware of my position, Thou dost witness my inner and outer being.

Grant Thy forgiveness unto me and unto the believers who responded to Thy Call. Be Thou my sufficing helper against the mischief of whosoever may desire to inflict sorrow upon me or wish me ill. Verily Thou art the Lord of all created things. Thou dost suffice everyone, while no one can be self-sufficient without Thee.

I IMPLORE Thee by the splendour of the light of Thy glorious face, the majesty of Thine ancient grandeur and the power of Thy transcendent sovereignty to ordain for us at this moment every measure of that which is good and seemly and to destine for us every portion of the outpourings of Thy grace. For granting of gifts doth not cause Thee loss, nor doth the bestowing of favours diminish Thy wealth.

[1] Qur'án 37:180–182

Glorified art Thou, O Lord! Verily I am poor while in truth Thou art rich; verily I am lowly while in truth Thou art mighty; verily I am impotent while in truth Thou art powerful; verily I am abased while in truth Thou art the most exalted; verily I am distressed while in truth Thou art the Lord of might.

D o Thou ordain for me, O Lord, every good thing Thou hast created or wilt create, and shield me from whatever evil Thou abhorrest from among the things Thou hast caused or wilt cause to exist. In truth Thy knowledge embraceth all things. Praised be Thou, verily no God is there but Thee, and nothing whatsoever in the heavens or on the earth and all that is between them can ever thwart Thy Purpose. Indeed potent art Thou over all things.

Far be it from the sublimity of Thy Being, O my God, that anyone seek Thy loving-kindness or favour. Far be it from Thy transcendent glory that anyone entreat Thee for the evidences of Thy bestowals and tender mercy. Too high art Thou for any soul to beseech the revelation of Thy gracious providence and loving care, and too sanctified is Thy glory for anyone to beg of Thee the outpourings of Thy blessings and of Thy heavenly bounty and grace. Throughout Thy kingdom of heaven and earth, which is endowed with manifold bounties, Thou art immeasurably glorified above aught whereunto any identity could be ascribed.

All that I beg of Thee, O my God, is to enable me, ere my soul departeth from my body, to attain Thy good-pleasure, even were it granted to me for a moment tinier than the infinitesimal fraction of a mustard seed. For if it departeth while Thou art pleased with me, then I shall be free from every concern or anxiety; but if it abandoneth me while Thou art displeased with me, then, even had I wrought every good deed, none would be of any avail, and had I earned every honour and glory, none would serve to exalt me.

I earnestly beseech Thee then, O my God, to graciously bestow Thy good-pleasure upon me when Thou dost cause me to ascend unto Thee and make me appear before Thy holy presence, inasmuch as Thou hast, from everlasting, been the God of immense bounty unto the people of Thy realm, and the Lord of most excellent gifts to all that dwell in the exalted heaven of Thine omnipotence.

How numerous the souls raised to life who were exposed to dire humiliation in Thy Path for exalting Thy Word and for glorifying Thy divine Unity! How profuse the blood that hath been shed for the sake of Thy Faith to vindicate the authenticity of Thy divine Mission and to celebrate Thy praise! How vast the possessions that were wrongfully seized in the Path of Thy love in order to affirm the loftiness of Thy sanctity and to extol Thy glorious Name! How many the feet that have trodden upon the dust in order to magnify Thy holy Word and to extol Thy glory! How innumerable the voices that were raised in lamentation, the hearts that were struck with terror, the grievous woes that none other than Thee can reckon, and the adversities and afflictions that remain inscrutable to anyone except Thyself; all this to establish, O my God, the loftiness of Thy sanctity and to demonstrate the transcendent character of Thy glory.

These decrees were ordained by Thee so that all created things might bear witness that they have been brought into being for the sake of naught else but Thee. Thou hast withheld from them the things that bring tranquillity to their hearts, that they might know of a certainty that whatever is associated with Thy holy Being is far superior to and exalted above aught else that would satisfy them; inasmuch as Thine indomitable power pervadeth all things, and nothing can ever frustrate it.

Indeed Thou hast caused these momentous happenings to come to pass that those who are endued with perception may readily recognize that they were ordained by Thee to demonstrate the loftiness of Thy divine Unity and to affirm the exaltation of Thy sanctity.

GLORY be unto Thee, O Lord! Although Thou mayest cause a person to be destitute of all earthly possessions, and from the beginning of his life until his ascension unto Thee he may be reduced to poverty through the operation of Thy decree, yet wert Thou to have brought him forth from the Tree of Thy love, such a bounty would indeed be far better for him than all the things Thou hast created in heaven and earth and whatsoever lieth between them; inasmuch as he will inherit the heavenly home, through the revelation of Thy favours, and will partake of the goodly gifts Thou hast provided therein; for the things which are with Thee are inexhaustible. This indeed is Thy blessing which according to the good-pleasure of Thy Will Thou dost bestow on those who tread the path of Thy love.

How numerous the souls who in former times were put to death for Thy sake, and in whose names all men now pride themselves; and how vast the number of those whom Thou didst enable to acquire earthly fortunes, and who amassed them while they were deprived of Thy Truth, and who in this day have passed into oblivion. Theirs is a grievous chastisement and a dire punishment.

O Lord! Provide for the speedy growth of the Tree of Thy divine Unity; water it then, O Lord, with the flowing waters of Thy good-pleasure, and cause it, before the revelations of Thy divine assurance, to yield such fruits as Thou desirest for Thy glorification and exaltation, Thy praise and thanksgiving, and to magnify Thy Name, to laud the oneness of Thine Essence and to offer adoration unto Thee, inasmuch as all this lieth within Thy grasp and in that of none other.

Great is the blessedness of those whose blood Thou hast chosen wherewith to water the Tree of Thine affirmation, and thus to exalt Thy holy and immutable Word.

Ordain for me, O my Lord, and for those who believe in Thee that which is deemed best for us in Thine estimation, as set forth in the Mother Book, for within the grasp of Thy hand Thou holdest the determined measures of all things.

Thy goodly gifts are unceasingly showered upon such as cherish Thy love and the wondrous tokens of Thy heavenly bounties are amply bestowed on those who recognize Thy divine Unity. We commit unto Thy care whatsoever Thou hast destined for us, and implore Thee to grant us all the good that Thy knowledge embraceth.

Protect me, O my Lord, from every evil that Thine omniscience perceiveth, inasmuch as there is no power nor strength but in Thee, no triumph is forthcoming save from

Thy presence, and it is Thine alone to command. Whatever God hath willed hath been, and that which He hath
not willed shall not be.

There is no power nor strength except in God, the Most
Exalted, the Most Mighty.

O LORD! Enable all the peoples of the earth to gain
admittance into the Paradise of Thy Faith, so that no
created being may remain beyond the bounds of Thy good-
pleasure.

From time immemorial Thou hast been potent to do
what pleaseth Thee and transcendent above whatsoever
Thou desirest.

VOUCHSAFE unto me, O my God, the full measure of
Thy love and Thy good-pleasure, and through the attrac-
tions of Thy resplendent light enrapture our hearts, O Thou
Who art the Supreme Evidence and the All-Glorified.
Send down upon me, as a token of Thy grace, Thy vitalizing
breezes, throughout the day-time and in the night season,
O Lord of bounty.

No deed have I done, O my God, to merit beholding
Thy face, and I know of a certainty that were I to live as
long as the world lasts I would fail to accomplish any deed
such as to deserve this favour, inasmuch as the station of a
servant shall ever fall short of access to Thy holy precincts,
unless Thy bounty should reach me and Thy tender mercy
pervade me and Thy loving-kindness encompass me.

All praise be unto Thee, O Thou besides Whom there is none other God. Graciously enable me to ascend unto Thee, to be granted the honour of dwelling in Thy nearness and to have communion with Thee alone. No God is there but Thee.

Indeed shouldst Thou desire to confer blessing upon a servant Thou wouldst blot out from the realm of his heart every mention or disposition except Thine Own mention; and shouldst Thou ordain evil for a servant by reason of that which his hands have unjustly wrought before Thy face, Thou wouldst test him with the benefits of this world and of the next that he might become preoccupied therewith and forget Thy remembrance.

GLORY be unto Thee, O Lord, Thou Who hast brought into being all created things, through the power of Thy behest.

O Lord! Assist those who have renounced all else but Thee, and grant them a mighty victory. Send down upon them, O Lord, the concourse of the angels in heaven and earth and all that is between, to aid Thy servants, to succour and strengthen them, to enable them to achieve success, to sustain them, to invest them with glory, to confer upon them honour and exaltation, to enrich them and to make them triumphant with a wondrous triumph.

Thou art their Lord, the Lord of the heavens and the earth, the Lord of all the worlds. Strengthen this Faith, O Lord, through the power of these servants and cause them to prevail over all the peoples of the world; for they, of a truth, are Thy servants who have detached themselves from aught else but Thee, and Thou verily art the protector of true believers.

Grant Thou, O Lord, that their hearts may, through allegiance to this, Thine inviolable Faith, grow stronger than anything else in the heavens and on earth and in whatsoever is between them; and strengthen, O Lord, their hands with the tokens of Thy wondrous power that they may manifest Thy power before the gaze of all mankind.

O Lord! Unto Thee I repair for refuge and toward all Thy signs I set my heart.

O Lord! Whether travelling or at home, and in my occupation or in my work, I place my whole trust in Thee.

Grant me then Thy sufficing help so as to make me independent of all things, O Thou Who art unsurpassed in Thy mercy!

Bestow upon me my portion, O Lord, as Thou pleasest, and cause me to be satisfied with whatsoever Thou hast ordained for me.

Thine is the absolute authority to command.

O Lord! Thou art the Remover of every anguish and the Dispeller of every affliction. Thou art He Who banisheth every sorrow and setteth free every slave, the Redeemer of every soul. O Lord! Grant deliverance through Thy mercy and reckon me among such servants of Thine as have gained salvation.

THROUGHOUT eternity Thou hast been, O my Lord, and wilt ever remain the One true God, while all else save Thee are needy and poor. Having clung tenaciously to Thy Cord, O my God, I have detached myself from all mankind, and having set my face towards the habitation of Thy tender mercy, I have turned away from all created things. Graciously inspire me, O my God, through Thy grace and bounty, Thy glory and majesty, and Thy dominion and grandeur, for no one mighty and all-knowing can I find beside Thee. Protect me, O my God, through the potency of Thy transcendent and all-sufficing glory and by the hosts of the heavens and the earth, inasmuch as in no one can I wholly place my trust but in Thee and no refuge is there but Thee.

Thou art God, my Lord, Thou knowest my needs, Thou seest my state and art well aware of what hath befallen me by reason of Thy decree, and of the earthly sufferings I have endured by Thy leave and as a token of Thy bounty and favour.

THE glory of glories and the most resplendent light rest upon Thee, O my God. Thy majesty is so transcendent that no human imagination can reach it and Thy consummate power is so sublime that the birds of men's hearts and minds can never attain its heights. All beings acknowledge their powerlessness to praise Thee as beseemeth Thy station. Immeasurably exalted art Thou. No one can glorify Thy Being, or fathom the evidences of Thy bounty as it exists in Thine inmost Essence, since Thou alone knowest Thyself as Thou art in Thyself.

I yield praise unto Thee, O Lord our God, for the bounty of having called into being the realm of creation and invention—a praise which shineth resplendent through the potency of Thine inspiration which none other but Thee can befittingly appraise. I glorify Thee moreover and render Thee thanks as beseemeth Thine awe-inspiring presence and the glory of Thine overpowering majesty, for this sublime blessing, this wondrous sign which is manifest in Thy kingdoms of Revelation and Creation.

All glory be unto Thee. Immeasurably exalted is that which beseemeth Thee. Verily no one hath ever adequately grasped the loftiness of Thy station, nor hath any one except Thee recognized Thee as beseemeth Thee. Thou art manifest through the outpourings of Thy bounty, while no one besides Thee can fathom the sublimity of Thy Revelation.

Magnified be Thy name. Hath aught else save Thee any independent existence so as to be capable of hinting at Thy nature, and doth anyone but Thee possess any trace of identity wherewith I could recognize Thee? All that is known owes its renown to the splendour of Thy Name, the Most Manifest, and every object is deeply stirred by the vibrating influence emanating from Thine invincible Will. Thou art nearer unto all things than all things.

Lauded and glorified art Thou. Too exalted is Thy loftiness for the hands of such as are endued with understanding to reach unto Thee, and too profound is Thy fathomless depth for the rivers of men's minds and perceptions to flow out therefrom.

In the Name of God, the Compassionate, the Merciful.

ALL praise be unto God Who was Ever-Existent ere created things were called into being, when there was no one else besides Him. He is the One Who hath been Ever-Abiding while no element of His creation did yet exist. Indeed the souls of them that are endued with understanding fail to comprehend the least manifestation of His attributes, and the minds of those who have acknowledged His unity are unable to perceive the most insignificant token of His omnipotence.

Sanctified art Thou, O Lord my God. The tongues of men fall short in extolling Thy glorious handiwork, how much more then would they falter in lauding the majesty of Thy transcendent power; and since human understanding is sore perplexed to fathom the mystery of a single object of Thy creation, how can anyone ever attain the recognition of Thine Own Being?

I have known Thee by Thy making known unto me that Thou art unknowable to anyone save Thyself. I have become apprised by the creation Thou hast fashioned out of sheer non-existence that the way to attain the comprehension of Thine Essence is barred to everyone. Thou art God, besides Whom there is none other God. No one except Thine Own Self can comprehend Thy nature. Thou art without peer or partner. From everlasting Thou hast been alone with no one else besides Thee and unto everlasting Thou wilt continue to be the same, while no created thing shall ever approach Thine exalted position.

All men, O my God, confess their powerlessness to know Thee as Thou knowest Thine Own Being; the generative impulse Thou hast released is manifest throughout the entire creation, and all created things which Thou hast fashioned are but expressions of Thy wondrous signs. Magnified be Thy name; Thou art immeasurably exalted above the strivings of anyone among Thy creatures to attain Thy recognition as is befitting and worthy of Thee.

Praise be unto Thee! The way in which Thou hast called into being Thy creation out of non-existence preventeth all created things from recognizing Thee, and the manner in which Thou hast fashioned the creatures, with the limitations imposed upon them, proclaimeth their utter nothingness before the revelations of Thine attributes.

Exalted art Thou, O my God! All mankind are powerless to celebrate Thy glory and the minds of men fall short of yielding praise unto Thee. I bear witness in Thy presence, O my God, that Thou art made known by Thy wondrous tokens and art recognized through the revelations of Thy signs. The fact that Thou hast brought us forth into existence prompteth me to acknowledge before Thee that Thou art immeasurably exalted above our praise, and by virtue of the qualities wherewith Thou hast endowed our beings I testify unto Thee that Thou art transcendent beyond our comprehension.

Grant that I may soar to the noblest heights in approaching Thee, and enable me to draw nigh unto Thee through the fragrance of Thy holiness. Thus may all impediments be dissolved by the light of ecstasy, and all remoteness from Thee be dissipated by my attainment unto the seats of reunion, and the subtle veils which have hindered me from entering Thy mansion of glory become so rarified that I may gain admittance into Thy presence, take up my abode near Thee, and voice the expressions of praise wherewith Thou hast described Thine Own Self unto me, bearing witness that Thou art God, that there is no God but Thee, the One, the Incomparable, the Ever-

Abiding, that Thou dost not beget, neither art Thou begotten, that Thou hast no offspring, no partner, nor is there any protector against humiliation but Thee, and Thou art the Lord of all worlds. I bear witness also that all besides Thee are but Thy creatures, and are held within Thy grasp. No one is favoured with means or liveth in want except by Thy Will. Thou art the King of everlasting days and the supreme Ruler. Thy might is potent over all things and all created things exist by Thy Will. All mankind recognize their lowly servitude and confess their shortcomings and naught is there which doth not celebrate Thy praise.

I beseech Thee, O my God, by the glory of Thy merciful Countenance and by the majesty of Thine ancient Name not to deprive me of the vitalizing fragrance of the evidences of Thy Days—such Days as Thou Thyself hast inaugurated and brought forth.

Thou art God, no God is there but Thee.

LAUDED and glorified art Thou, O Lord my God! Thou art supreme over the realm of being and Thy power pervadeth all created things. Thou holdest the kingdom of creation within Thy grasp and dost call into being in conformity with Thy pleasure.

All praise be unto Thee, O Lord my God! I beseech Thee by such souls as are eagerly waiting at Thy gate and by those holy beings who have attained the court of Thy presence, to cast upon us the glances of Thy tender compassion and to regard us with the eye of Thy loving providence. Cause our souls to be enkindled with the fire of Thy tender affection and give us to drink of the living waters of Thy bounty. Keep us steadfast in the path of Thine ardent love and enable us to abide within the precincts of Thy holiness. Verily Thou art the Giver, the Most Generous, the All-Knowing, the All-Informed.

Glorified art Thou, O my God! I invoke Thee by Thy Most Great Name through which the hidden secrets of God, the Most Exalted, were divulged and the kindreds of all nations converged toward the focal centre of faith and certitude, through which Thy luminous Words streamed forth for the quickening of mankind and the essence of all knowledge was revealed from that Embodiment of bounty. May my life, my inmost being, my soul and my body be offered up as a sacrifice for the dust ennobled by His footsteps.

I earnestly beg Thee, O Lord my God, by Thy most glorious Name whereby Thy sovereignty hath been established and the tokens of Thy might have been manifested, and whereby the oceans of life and of holy ecstasy have surged for the reviving of the mouldering bones of all Thy creatures and for the stirring of the limbs of such as have embraced Thy Cause—I earnestly beg Thee to graciously ordain for us the good of this world and of the next, to enable us to gain admission into the court of Thy mercy and loving-kindness and to kindle in our hearts the fire of joy and ecstasy in such wise that the hearts of all men may thereby be attracted.

Verily Thou art the All-Powerful, the Protector, the Almighty, the Self-Subsisting.

GLORY be unto Thee, O Lord my God! I beg Thee to forgive me and those who support Thy Faith. Verily Thou art the sovereign Lord, the Forgiver, the Most Generous. O my God! Enable such servants of Thine as are deprived of knowledge to be admitted into Thy Cause; for once they learn of Thee, they bear witness to the truth of the Day of Judgement and do not dispute the revelations of Thy bounty. Send down upon them the tokens of Thy grace and grant them, wherever they reside, a liberal share of that which Thou hast ordained for the pious among Thy servants. Thou art in truth the Supreme Ruler, the All-Bounteous, the Most Benevolent.

O my God! Let the outpourings of Thy bounty and blessings descend upon homes whose inmates have embraced Thy Faith, as a token of Thy grace and as a mark of loving-kindness from Thy presence. Verily unsurpassed art Thou in granting forgiveness. Should Thy bounty be withheld from anyone, how could he be reckoned among the followers of the Faith in Thy Day?

Bless me, O my God, and those who will believe in Thy signs on the appointed Day, and such as cherish my love in their hearts—a love which Thou dost instil into them. Verily Thou art the Lord of righteousness, the Most Exalted.

IMMEASURABLY exalted art Thou, O my God, above the endeavours of all beings and created things to praise Thee and recognize Thee. No creature can ever comprehend Thee as beseemeth the reality of Thy holy Being and no servant can ever worship Thee as is worthy of Thine unknowable Essence. Praise be unto Thee; too high is Thine exalted Self for any allusions proceeding from Thy creatures ever to gain access unto Thy presence.

Whenever, O my God, I soared into Thy holy atmosphere and attained the inmost spirit of prayerfulness unto Thee, I was led to recognize that Thou art inaccessible and that no mention of Thee can ever reach Thy transcendent court. Therefore I turn towards Thy Loved Ones—They upon Whom Thou hast graciously conferred Thine Own station that They might manifest Thy love and Thy true knowledge. Bless Them then, O my God, with every distinction and goodly gift which Thy knowledge may reckon within the domain of Thy power.

O my God, my Lord and my Master! I swear by Thy might and glory that Thou alone and no one else besides Thee art the ultimate Desire of all men, and that Thou alone and none other save Thee art the Object of adoration. O my God! The paths of Thine inaccessible glory have prompted me to voice these words and the ways of Thine unattainable heights have guided me to make these allusions. Exalted art Thou, O my God! The evidences of Thy revelation are too manifest for me to need to refer to aught else save Thyself, and the love I cherish for Thee is far sweeter to my taste than the knowledge of all things and freeth me from the need to seek anyone's knowledge other than Thine.

All praise be unto Thee, O my Lord. I verily believe in Thee, as Thou art in Thyself; and of Thee, as Thou art in Thyself, I beg forgiveness for myself and on behalf of all mankind.

O my God! Wholly have I fled unto Thy face and have cast myself before Thee and no power have I over aught in Thy holy presence. Shouldst Thou chastise me with Thy might, Thou wouldst assuredly be just in Thy decree; and wert Thou to bestow every goodly gift on me, Thou wouldst indeed be most generous and bountiful. Verily Thou art independent of all the peoples of the world.

I have sought reunion with Thee, O my Master, yet have I failed to attain thereto save through the knowledge of detachment from aught save Thee. I have yearned for Thy love, but failed to find it except in renouncing everything other than Thyself. I have been eager to worship Thee, yet have I failed to achieve Thy adoration, except by loving those who cherish Thy love. No one do I recognize, O my God, except Thee. Thou art incomparable and hast no partner. Thou alone knowest our shortcomings and none other hath this knowledge. I beg Thy forgiveness for whatever doth displease Thee.

I call upon Thee at all times with the tongue of Thine inspiration, saying: 'Thou art in truth the All-Possessing, the Peerless. No God is there but Thee. Immeasurably far and exalted art Thou above the descriptions of those who arrogantly assign peers unto Thee.'

ALL majesty and glory, O my God, and all dominion and light and grandeur and splendour be unto Thee. Thou bestowest sovereignty on whom Thou willest and dost withhold it from whom Thou desirest. No God is there but Thee, the All-Possessing, the Most Exalted. Thou art He Who createth from naught the universe and all that dwell therein. There is nothing worthy of Thee except Thyself, while all else but Thee are as outcasts in Thy holy presence and are as nothing when compared to the glory of Thine Own Being.

Far be it from me to extol Thy virtues save by what Thou hast extolled Thyself in Thy weighty Book where Thou sayest, 'No vision taketh in Him but He taketh in all vision. He is the Subtile, the All-Perceiving.'[1] Glory be unto Thee, O my God, indeed no mind or vision, however keen or discriminating, can ever grasp the nature of the most insignificant of Thy signs. Verily Thou art God, no God is there besides Thee. I bear witness that Thou Thyself alone art the sole expression of Thine attributes, that the praise of no one besides Thee can ever attain to Thy holy court nor can Thine attributes ever be fathomed by anyone other than Thyself.

Glory be unto Thee, Thou art exalted above the description of anyone save Thyself, since it is beyond human conception to befittingly magnify Thy virtues or to comprehend the inmost reality of Thine Essence. Far be it from Thy glory that Thy creatures should describe Thee or that any one besides Thyself should ever know Thee. I have known Thee, O my God, by reason of Thy making Thyself known unto me, for hadst Thou not revealed Thyself unto me, I would not have known Thee. I worship Thee by virtue of Thy summoning me unto Thee, for had it not been for Thy summons I would not have worshipped Thee. Lauded art Thou, O my God, my trespasses have waxed mighty and my sins have assumed grievous proportions. How disgraceful my plight will prove to be in Thy holy presence. I have failed to know Thee to the extent Thou didst reveal Thyself unto me; I have failed to worship Thee with a devotion worthy of Thy summons; I have failed to obey Thee through not treading the path of Thy love in the manner Thou didst inspire me.

Thy might beareth me witness, O my God, what

[1] Qur'án 6:103

befitteth Thee is far greater and more exalted than any being could attempt to accomplish. Indeed nothing can ever comprehend Thee as is worthy of Thee nor can any servile creature worship Thee as beseemeth Thine adoration. So perfect and comprehensive is Thy proof, O my God, that its inner essence transcendeth the description of any soul and so abundant are the outpourings of Thy gifts that no faculty can appraise their infinite range.

O my God! O my Master! I beseech Thee by Thy manifold bounties and by the pillars which sustain Thy throne of glory, to have pity on these lowly people who are powerless to bear the unpleasant things of this fleeting life, how much less then can they bear Thy chastisement in the life to come—a chastisement which is ordained by Thy justice, called forth by Thy wrath and will continue to exist for ever.

I beg Thee by Thyself, O my God, my Lord and my Master, to intercede in my behalf. I have fled from Thy justice unto Thy mercy. For my refuge I am seeking Thee and such as turn not away from Thy path, even for a twinkling of an eye—they for whose sake Thou didst create the creation as a token of Thy grace and bounty.

O MY God! There is no one but Thee to allay the anguish of my soul, and Thou art my highest aspiration, O my God. My heart is wedded to none save Thee and such as Thou dost love. I solemnly declare that my life and death are both for Thee. Verily Thou art incomparable and hast no partner.

O my Lord! I beg Thee to forgive me for shutting myself out from Thee. By Thy glory and majesty, I have failed to befittingly recognize Thee and to worship Thee, while Thou dost make Thyself known unto me and callest me to remembrance as beseemeth Thy station. Grievous woe would betide me, O my Lord, wert Thou to take hold of me by reason of my misdeeds and trespasses. No helper do I know of other than Thee. No refuge do I have to flee to save Thee. None among Thy creatures can dare to intercede with Thyself without Thy leave. I hold fast to Thy love before Thy court, and, according to Thy bidding, I earnestly pray unto Thee as befitteth Thy glory. I beg Thee to heed my call as Thou hast promised me. Verily Thou art God; no God is there but Thee. Alone and un-aided, Thou art independent of all created things. Neither can the devotion of Thy lovers profit Thee, nor the evil doings of the faithless harm Thee. Verily Thou art my God, He Who will never fail in His promise.

O my God! I beseech Thee by the evidences of Thy favour, to let me draw nigh to the sublime heights of Thy holy presence, and protect me from inclining myself to-ward the subtle allusions of aught else but Thee. Guide my steps, O my God, unto that which is acceptable and pleas-ing to Thee. Shield me, through Thy might, from the fury of Thy wrath and chastisement, and hold me back from entering habitations not desired by Thee.

O MY God! I have failed to know Thee as is worthy of Thy glory, and I have failed to fear Thee as befitteth my station. How can I make mention of Thee when I am in this condition, and how can I set my face towards Thee when I have fallen short of my duty in worshipping Thee?

Thou didst not call me into being to demonstrate the potency of Thy might which is unmistakably manifest and evident; for Thou art God Who everlastingly existed when there was naught. Rather Thou didst create us through Thy transcendent power that a bare mention may be graciously made of us before the resplendent manifestation of Thy Remembrance.

I have no knowledge of Thee, O my God, but that which Thou hast taught me whereby I might recognize Thy Self—a knowledge which reflecteth only my failure and sinfulness. Here am I then, O my God, wholly consecrated unto Thee, willing to do what Thou desirest. Humbly I cast myself before the revelations of Thy mercy, confessing that Thou art God, no God is there but Thee, and that Thou art incomparable, hast no partner and naught is there like Thee. Unto this Thou Thyself bearest witness, as well becometh Thy glory.

He is God, the Sovereign Ruler, the Ever-Living,
He Whose help all men implore.

LAUDED and glorified art Thou, O Lord! Both the world of existence and the souls of men bear witness that Thou art transcendent above the revelations of Thy handiwork, and the bearers of Thy names and attributes proclaim that Thou art immeasurably exalted above such praise as the dwellers of the dominions of creation and invention may render unto Thee. All appearances and realities indicate the oneness of Thine Essence, and all evidences and signs reflect the truth that Thou art God and there is no peer or partner for Thee throughout the kingdoms of heaven and earth.

Immensely high and sanctified art Thou, O Lord! Thy divine Being testifieth that Thou art inscrutable to all that dwell in Thy realm of existence, and Thine inmost Essence proclaimeth that Thou art far above the description of those who reveal Thy glory.

The signs which the sanctified essences reveal and the words which the exalted realities express and the allusions manifested by the ethereal entities all proclaim that Thou art immeasurably exalted above the reach of the embodiments of the realm of being, and all solemnly affirm that Thou art immensely high above the description of such as are wrapt in the veils of fancy.

Praise be unto Thee, O Lord! Thy divine Being is a sure testimony of the oneness of Thine inmost Essence and Thy supreme divinity beareth witness to the unity of Thy Self, and the realities of all created things testify that no tie of intercourse bindeth Thee to anything in the kingdom of creation which Thou hast fashioned.

Every man of perception who hath scaled the noble heights of detachment, and every man of eloquence who hath attained the most sublime station, beareth witness that Thou art God, the Incomparable, and that Thou hast assigned no associate unto Thyself in the kingdom of creation, nor is there anyone to compare with Thee in the realm of invention. Men of wisdom, who had but a notion of the revelation of Thy glory, conceived a likeness of Thee according to their own understanding, and men of erudition, who had gained but a glimpse of the manifold evidences of Thy loving-kindness and glory, have contrived peers for Thee in conformity with their own imaginations.

Glorified, immeasurably glorified art Thou, O Lord!

Every man of insight is far astray in his attempt to recognize Thee, and every man of consummate learning is sore perplexed in his search after Thee. Every evidence falleth short of Thine unknowable Essence and every light retreateth and sinketh below the horizon when confronted with but a glimmer of the dazzling splendour of Thy might.

Bestow on me, O my Lord, Thy gracious bounty and benevolent gifts and grant me that which beseemeth the sublimity of Thy glory. Aid me, O my Lord, to achieve a singular victory. Open Thou the door of unfailing success before me and grant that the things Thou hast promised may be close at hand. Thou art in truth potent over all things. Refresh my heart, O my God, with the living waters of Thy love and give me a draught, O my Master, from the chalice of Thy tender mercy. Let me abide, O my Lord, within the habitation of Thy glory, and suffer me, O my God, to emerge from the darkness in which Thy divine obscurity is shrouded. Enable me to partake of every good Thou hast vouchsafed unto Him Who is the Point and unto such as are the exponents of His Cause, and ordain for me that which beseemeth Thee and well becometh Thy station. Do Thou graciously forgive me for the things that I have wrought in Thy holy presence, and look not upon me with the glance of justice, but rather deliver me through Thy grace, treat me with Thy mercy and deal with me according to Thy bountiful favours, as is worthy of Thy glory.

Thou art the Ever-Forgiving, the All-Glorious, the Bestower of favours and gifts, the Lord of grace abounding. Verily no God is there but Thee. Thou art the All-Possessing, the Most High.

Sanctified art Thou, O Lord, Thou unto Whom all render thanksgiving. Whatever I may affirm of Thee would be but a wanton crime before Thee, and whatever mention I may choose to make of Thee would be the essence of transgression, and whatever the praise whereby I may glorify Thee, it would amount to sheer blasphemy. No one else besides Thee hath been or will ever be able to fathom Thy mystery, neither hath any one succeeded nor will anyone succeed at any time in discovering Thine Essence.

Magnified art Thou! No God is there but Thee. Thou art in truth the Supreme Ruler, the Help in Peril, the Most High, the Incomparable, the Omnipotent, the All-Powerful. Verily Thou art mighty in Thy prowess, the Lord of transcendent glory and majesty.

Protect Thou, O God, whosoever learneth this prayer by heart and reciteth it in the day-time and in the night season. Verily Thou art God, the Lord of creation, the All-Sufficing. Thou art faithful to Thy promise and doest whatsoever Thou pleasest. Thou art the One Who holdeth in His hands the dominions of earth and heaven. Verily Thou art the Almighty, the Inaccessible, the Help in Peril, the All-Compelling.

O my God, my Lord and my Master! I have detached myself from my kindred and have sought through Thee to become independent of all that dwell on earth and ever ready to receive that which is praiseworthy in Thy sight. Bestow on me such good as will make me independent of aught else but Thee, and grant me an ampler share of Thy boundless favours. Verily Thou art the Lord of grace abounding.

I ADJURE Thee by Thy might, O my God! Let no harm beset me in times of tests, and in moments of heedlessness guide my steps aright through Thine inspiration. Thou art God, potent art Thou to do what Thou desirest. No one can withstand Thy Will or thwart Thy Purpose.

I BEG Thy forgiveness, O my God, and implore pardon after the manner Thou wishest Thy servants to direct themselves to Thee. I beg of Thee to wash away our sins as befitteth Thy Lordship, and to forgive me, my parents, and those who in Thy estimation have entered the abode of Thy love in a manner which is worthy of Thy transcendent sovereignty and well beseemeth the glory of Thy celestial power.

O my God! Thou hast inspired my soul to offer its supplication to Thee, and but for Thee, I would not call upon Thee. Lauded and glorified art Thou; I yield Thee praise inasmuch as Thou didst reveal Thyself unto me, and I beg Thee to forgive me, since I have fallen short in my duty to know Thee and have failed to walk in the path of Thy love.

LAUDED be Thy Name, O Lord our God! Thou art in truth the Knower of things unseen. Ordain for us such good as Thine all-embracing knowledge can measure. Thou art the sovereign Lord, the Almighty, the Best Beloved.

All praise be unto Thee, O Lord! We shall seek Thy grace on the appointed Day and shall put our whole reliance in Thee, Who art our Lord. Glorified art Thou, O God! Grant us that which is good and seemly that we may be able to dispense with everything but Thee. Verily Thou art the Lord of all worlds.

O God! Recompense those who endure patiently in Thy days and strengthen their hearts to walk undeviatingly in the path of Truth. Grant then, O Lord, such goodly gifts as would enable them to gain admittance into Thy blissful Paradise. Exalted art Thou, O Lord God. Let Thy heavenly blessings descend upon homes whose inmates have believed in Thee. Verily, unsurpassed art Thou in sending down divine blessings. Send forth, O God, such hosts as would render Thy faithful servants victorious. Thou dost fashion the created things through the power of Thy decree as Thou pleasest. Thou art in truth the Sovereign, the Creator, the All-Wise.

Say: God is indeed the Maker of all things. He giveth sustenance in plenty to whomsoever He willeth. He is the Creator, the Source of all beings, the Fashioner, the Almighty, the Maker, the All-Wise. He is the Bearer of the most excellent titles throughout the heavens and the earth and whatever lieth between them. All do His bidding, and all the dwellers of earth and heaven celebrate His praise, and unto Him shall all return.

THROUGH Thy revelation, O my God, Thou hast enabled me to know Thee, and through the radiance of Thine effulgent splendour Thou hast inspired me with Thy remembrance. Thou art the One nearest to me with naught else between Thee and me, and Thou art the One Whose power nothing whatsoever can frustrate. Far be it then from Thine Essence that the mightiest birds of the souls of men or of human imaginings should ever scale its heights, and too exalted is Thy holy Being for the loftiest sentiments of men of understanding to attain unto Thee. From everlasting no one hath comprehended Thine Own Self, and unto everlasting Thou shalt remain what Thou hast been since time immemorial with no one else besides Thee.

Magnified be Thy Name, Thou art the Best Beloved Who hast enabled me to know Thee and Thou art that All-Renowned One Who hast graciously favoured me with Thy love. Thou art the Ancient of Days Whom none can ever describe through the evidences of Thy glory and majesty, and Thou art the mighty One Whom none can ever comprehend through the revelations of Thy greatness and beauty, inasmuch as the expressions of majesty and grandeur and the attributes of dominion and beauty are but the tokens of Thy divine Will and the effulgent reflections of Thy sovereignty which, by reason of their very essence and nature, proclaim that the way is barred and bear witness that the pathway is inaccessibly beyond the reach of men.

In the Name of Thy Lord, the Creator, the Sovereign, the All-Sufficing, the Most Exalted, He Whose help is implored by all men.

SAY: O my God! O Thou Who art the Maker of the

heavens and of the earth, O Lord of the Kingdom! Thou well knowest the secrets of my heart, while Thy Being is inscrutable to all save Thyself. Thou seest whatsoever is of me, while no one else can do this save Thee. Vouchsafe unto me, through Thy grace, what will enable me to dispense with all except Thee, and destine for me that which will make me independent of everyone else besides Thee. Grant that I may reap the benefit of my life in this world and in the next. Open to my face the portals of Thy grace and graciously confer upon me Thy tender mercy and bestowals.

O Thou Who art the Lord of grace abounding! Let Thy celestial aid surround those who love Thee and bestow upon us the gifts and the bounties Thou dost possess. Be Thou sufficient unto us of all things, forgive our sins and have mercy upon us. Thou art Our Lord and the Lord of all created things. No one else do we invoke but Thee and naught do we beseech but Thy favours. Thou art the Lord of bounty and grace, invincible in Thy power and the most skilful in Thy designs. No God is there but Thee, the All-Possessing, the Most Exalted.

Confer Thy blessings, O my Lord, upon the Messengers, the holy ones and the righteous. Verily Thou art God, the Peerless, the All-Compelling.

GLORIFIED art Thou, O Lord my God! Thou art in truth the King of kings. Thou dost confer sovereignty upon whomsoever Thou willest and dost seize it from whomsoever Thou willest. Thou dost exalt whomsoever Thou willest and dost abase whomsoever Thou willest. Thou dost render victorious whomsoever Thou willest and dost bring humiliation upon whomsoever Thou willest. Thou dost bestow wealth upon whomsoever Thou willest and dost reduce to poverty whomsoever Thou willest. Thou dost cause whomsoever Thou willest to prevail over whomsoever Thou willest. Within Thy grasp Thou dost hold the empire of all created things and through the potency of Thy sovereign behest Thou dost call into being whomsoever Thou willest. Verily Thou art the Omniscient, the Omnipotent, the Lord of power.

PRAISED and glorified art Thou, O God! Grant that the day of attaining Thy holy presence may be fast approaching. Cheer our hearts through the potency of Thy love and good-pleasure and bestow upon us steadfastness that we may willingly submit to Thy Will and Thy Decree. Verily Thy knowledge embraceth all the things Thou hast created or wilt create and Thy celestial might transcendeth whatsoever Thou hast called or wilt call into being. There is none to be worshipped but Thee, there is none to be desired except Thee, there is none to be adored besides Thee and there is naught to be loved save Thy good-pleasure.

Verily Thou art the supreme Ruler, the Sovereign Truth, the Help in Peril, the Self-Subsisting.

THOU knowest full well, O my God, that tribulations have showered upon me from all directions and that no one can dispel or transmute them except Thee. I know of a certainty, by virtue of my love for Thee, that Thou wilt never cause tribulations to befall any soul unless Thou desirest to exalt his station in Thy celestial Paradise and to buttress his heart in this earthly life with the bulwark of Thine all-compelling power, that it may not become inclined toward the vanities of this world. Indeed Thou art well aware that under all conditions I would cherish the remembrance of Thee far more than the ownership of all that is in the heavens and on the earth.

Strengthen my heart, O my God, in Thine obedience and in Thy love and grant that I may be clear of the entire company of Thine adversaries. Verily I swear by Thy glory that I yearn for naught besides Thyself, nor do I desire anything except Thy mercy, nor am I apprehensive of aught save Thy justice. I beg Thee to forgive me as well as those whom Thou lovest, howsoever Thou pleasest. Verily Thou art the Almighty, the Bountiful.

Immensely exalted art Thou, O Lord of the heavens and earth, above the praise of all men, and may peace be upon Thy faithful servants and glory be unto God, the Lord of all the worlds.

PRAISE be to Thee, O Lord, my Best Beloved! Make me steadfast in Thy Cause and grant that I may be reckoned among those who have not violated Thy Covenant nor followed the gods of their own idle fancy. Enable me, then, to obtain a seat of truth in Thy presence, bestow upon me a token of Thy mercy and let me join with such of Thy servants as shall have no fear nor shall they be put to grief.

Abandon me not to myself, O my Lord, nor deprive me of recognizing Him Who is the Manifestation of Thine Own Self, nor account me with such as have turned away from Thy holy presence. Number me, O my God, with those who are privileged to fix their gaze upon Thy Beauty and who take such delight therein that they would not exchange a single moment thereof with the sovereignty of the kingdom of heavens and earth or with the entire realm of creation. Have mercy on me, O Lord, in these days when the peoples of Thine earth have erred grievously; supply me then, O my God, with that which is good and seemly in Thine estimation. Thou art verily the All-Powerful, the Gracious, the Bountiful, the Ever-Forgiving.

Grant, O my God, that I may not be reckoned among those whose ears are deaf, whose eyes are blind, whose tongues are speechless and whose hearts have failed to comprehend. Deliver me, O Lord, from the fire of ignorance and of selfish desire, suffer me to be admitted into the precincts of Thy transcendent mercy and send down upon me that which Thou hast ordained for Thy chosen ones. Potent art Thou to do what Thou willest. Verily Thou art the Help in Peril, the Self-Subsisting.

O MY God, O my Lord, O my Master! I beg Thee to forgive me for seeking any pleasure save Thy love, or any comfort except Thy nearness, or any delight besides Thy good-pleasure, or any existence other than communion with Thee.

Thou seest, O my Lord, my dwelling-place in the heart of this mountain and Thou dost witness my forbearance. Verily I have desired naught else but Thy love and the love of those who love Thee. How can I extol the effulgent beauty of Thy Lordship, conscious as I am of my nothingness before the habitation of Thy glory? Yet the sorrow of solitude and loneliness prompteth me to invoke Thee through this prayer, perchance Thy trusted servants may become aware of my lamentations, may supplicate unto Thee on my behalf, and Thou wouldst graciously answer their prayers as a token of Thy grace and Thy favour. I bear witness that there is no God but Thee, inasmuch as Thou art invested with sovereignty, grandeur, glory and power which no one among Thy servants can visualize or comprehend. Indeed Thou shalt, by virtue of that which is inherent in Thine Essence, ever remain inscrutable unto all except Thyself.

Is there any Remover of difficulties save God? Say: Praised be God! He is God! All are His servants and all abide by His bidding!

NOTES

PASSAGES TRANSLATED BY SHOGHI EFFENDI

A considerable number of passages from the Writings of the Báb
were translated by Shoghi Effendi and quoted in his various works.
Those included in this compilation are listed below.

page   line

87   7   'How veiled are ye, O My creatures, . . .' to '. . . refuse
              Him even a lamp!'

101   6   'The Bayán is from beginning . . .' to '. . . both His
              fire and His light.'

104   3   'a thousand perusals of the Bayán . . .' to '. . . God
              shall make manifest.'

105   27   'It is clear and evident . . .' to '. . . had no beginning
              and will have no end.'

108   1   'today the Bayán is . . .' to '. . . perfection will become
              apparent.'

117   12   'Gracious God!'

117   13   'seven powerful sovereigns . . .' to '. . . traces of their
              names.'

123   21   'The blame falleth upon their doctors . . .' to '. . . and
              attain unto salvation!'

155   15   'Consecrate Thou, O my God, . . .' to '. . . nor shall it
              return unto Me.'

156   4   'He—glorified be His mention . . .' to '. . . is nigh,
              ready to answer.'

168   21   'O congregation of the Bayán . . .' to '. . . is the Help
              in Peril, the Most High.'

217   18   'Is there any Remover of difficulties . . .' to '. . . abide
              by His bidding!'

Translations from the Writings of the Báb made by Shoghi Effendi,
but not included in this compilation, may be found in *God Passes
By* on pages 25, 29 and 30; in *The World Order of Bahá'u'lláh* on
pages 100, 101, 126 and 127; and in the *Epistle to the Son of the Wolf*
on pages 141, 142, 151 to 160, 165, and 171 to 176.